# LEARNING FROM
# WOLVES

*Lessons for Humans from
Plant and Animal Life*

## Sara Hines Martin MRE, MS

WESTBOW
PRESS
A DIVISION OF THOMAS NELSON

WestBow Press books may be ordered through booksellers or by contacting:

WestBow Press
A Division of Thomas Nelson
1663 Liberty Drive
Bloomington, IN 47403
www.westbowpress.com
1-(866) 928-1240

Because of the dynamic nature of the Internet, any web addresses or links contained in this book may have changed since publication and may no longer be valid. The views expressed in this work are solely those of the author and do not necessarily reflect the views of the publisher, and the publisher hereby disclaims any responsibility for them.

Any people depicted in stock imagery provided by Thinkstock are models, and such images are being used for illustrative purposes only. Certain stock imagery © Thinkstock.

Scripture marked New International Version is taken from the Holy Bible, New International Version®. Copyright © 1973, 1978, 1984 Biblica. Used by permission of Zondervan. All rights reserved.

Scripture marked King James Version is taken from the King James Version of the Bible.

ISBN: 978-1-4497-6817-1 (sc)
ISBN: 978-1-4497-6818-8 (e)

Library of Congress Control Number: 2012917516

Printed in the United States of America

WestBow Press rev. date: 9/19/2012

# LEARNING FROM WOLVES

Also by Sara Hines Martin

*Frente al Cancer: Un Gigante a Mi Lado.*
*Healing for Adult Children of Alcoholics*
*Shame On You! Help for Adults from Alcoholic and Other Shame-Bound Families*
*Meeting Needs Through Support Groups*
*More Than Petticoats: Remarkable Georgia Women*
*Stepping Up to Spiritual Maturity: The Stages of Faith Development*
*Shakin' Up the Kingdom: Princess Lucinda Becomes the Queen*

# LEARNING FROM WOLVES

Lessons for Humans from Plants and Animals

Sara Hines Martin, MRE, MS
Author of *Stepping Up to Spiritual Maturity*

# Contents

# Preface

In the beginning God created the heavens and the earth....
Genesis 1:1 (*The Holy Bible,* New International Version)
Then God said, "Let the land produce vegetation:
seed-bearing plants and trees on the land that bear
fruit with seed in it, according to their various kinds."
And it was so. The land produced vegetation: plants
bearing seed according to their kinds and trees bearing
fruit with seed in it according to their kinds.
*And God saw that it was good.*
Genesis 1:11, 12 (*The Holy Bible,* New International Version)

And God said, "Let the water teem with living creatures, and
let birds fly above the earth across the expanse of the sky." So
God created the great creatures of the sea and every living
and moving thing with which the water teems, according to
their kinds, and every winged bird according to its kind.
*And God saw that it was good.*
Genesis 1:20, 21 (*The Holy Bible,* New International Version)

And God said, "Let the land produce living creatures according
to their kinds: livestock, creatures that move along the ground,
and wild animals, each according to its kind." And it was so....
*And God saw that it was good.*
Genesis 1:24, 25b (*The Holy Bible,* New International Version)

Then God said, "Let us make man in
our image, in our likeness,
And let them rule over the fish of the
sea and the birds of the air,
over the livestock, over all the earth, and over
all the creatures that move along the ground."
So God created man in his own image....
*And God saw that it was good.*
Genesis 1:26, 27a (*The Holy Bible,* New International Version)

Then God said, "I give you every seed-bearing plant on the face
of the whole earth and every tree that has fruit with seed in it.
They will be yours for food.
And to all the beasts of the earth and all the birds of the air
and all the creatures that move on the ground—
every thing that has the breath of life in it—
I give every green plant for food. And it was so.
*God saw all that he had made, and it was very good.*
Genesis 1:29, 30, 31a (*The Holy Bible,*
New International Version)

# Introduction:

Did you know? "When food is scarce, wolves give birth to fewer pups, sometimes none at all, if they are starving," wrote Jean Craighead George.

"Panthers will regulate their own numbers according to the size of the area...when an area is well stocked with panther, then fewer are born," wrote James P. McMullen.

Sigurd F. Olson wrote: "An overly aggressive beaver colony can eat itself out of house and home if it disregards the basic rules of population and survival. On one of my favorite trout streams...a beaver colony moved in to harvest all the aspen and birch within reach....and before long a dam was built across the lower end of the stream, backing up the water several feet, with a huge house midway upstream. It was impossible to wade because of the depth and deposition of black silt over the old hard bed of sand and gravel I had known. In a few years the aspen and birch were gone, but that did not deter the beavers, for then they started on the fringing border of alder and dwarf birch and willow, until the entire flat was practically denuded of vegetation. Their canals ran far into the woods and to step into one meant going down into a boggy hole often waist deep. Finally—and this took about ten years—there was no more food except on the distant hillside beyond the reach of the canals. Only then did the beavers leave."

He also related that moose can also eat themselves out of forage, as they did on Isle Royale before a pack of wolves moved in one winter on the ice. The moose had eaten the balsams and cedars almost down to the ground and the moose were rapidly dying of starvation. With a pack of wolves to keep them in check, the browse has come back and the pack has not increased, a classic example of population in balance.

He told about deer, on the Kaibab Plateau of Arizona, without the presence of predators, soon reached such proportions they were dying by hundreds and thousands before hunting was allowed. *"And so it is everywhere: the freedom of the wilderness demands its own controls or disaster results,"* he wrote. (italics added).

What good lessons for human beings! Since I am a psychotherapist, I immediately thought of all the human beings who bring babies into the world even though they do not have the resources to support them. I often hear the statistics regarding the number of babies born in my state who become the responsibility of the state.

*What amazing information,* I thought. The above quotes gripped me to the extent that I began to research other lessons human beings can learn from plant and animal life. I give these stories to you and know that each of you will respond in your own way. I hope you receive inspiration from them, and if they inspire you to action, I have accomplished my purpose in writing the book.

# Chapter One

# We're All Connected

God sets the lonely in families....
Psalm 68:1 (*The Holy Bible*, New International Version)

## We need community

As Dr. Betty Siegel celebrated her twentieth year as president of Kennesaw State University in Kennesaw, Georgia, a group of friends donated five giant sequoia seedlings to be planted on the campus in her honor.

Why did they choose five instead of only one or two? *Research shows that trees cannot survive in isolation; they must have a community.* The trees cluster together, actually supporting each other. As their roots entangle, this network provides them fortification during raging storms and floods. This leads to the sequoia's longevity, some living to be more than 1,000 years old.

## Trees are like people

In *The Orchard*, Jeffrey Stepakoff wrote: "...like many people in Gilmer County, Roswell Culpepper planted apple trees. He planted both Rome Beauty and Golden Delicious as saplings, roots balled and burlapped, careful to place the two cultivars near each other in the orchard, as apple trees are self-incompatible, in that a single type will not pollinate itself, no matter how many bees scatter pollen among its blossoms. It takes at least two trees of different varieties to create a productive orchard, and...Ros Culpepper understood this well. *An apple tree is just like a person,* he was fond of saying. In order to thrive, it needs companionship that's similar to it in some ways, but quite different in others.

### They never desert the flock

In Ron Rash's novel, *The Cove,* Laurel, a girl who lives in western North Carolina, admired the parakeet's song. "She remembered how Becky Dobbins, a store owner's daughter, asked why the farmer killed such a pretty bird. Because they'll eat your apples and cherries, Riley Watkins had answered from the back row (of the classroom). Anyway, they're the stupidest things you ever seen, Riley added, and told how his daddy fired into a flock and the unharmed parakeets didn't fly away but kept circling until not one was left alive. Miss Calicut (the teacher) had shaken her head. It's not because they're stupid, Riley.

"They never desert the flock, Miss Calicut had told them."

### Helping others of the flock

Even if the following story may be an urban legend, it is very heart warming:

A flock of ducks landed on a northern lake in winter. The next morning, trapped in the ice, they could not fly away. Another flock of ducks flew over and landed in between the trapped ducks. The heat of the ducks' bodies melted the ice so that the imprisoned ducks were able to fly away.

### What if we flew in formation?

All of us have watched a flock of geese in formation flying overhead in its V formation and marveled and asked, "How do they do it?"

As each goose flaps its wings, it creates an uplift for the

following bird. In a V formation, the whole flock adds at least 71% more flying range than if each flew alone. Whenever a goose falls out of formation, it feels the drag and resistance of trying to fly alone, and quickly gets back into formation. When a goose gets tired, it rotates back into the formation, and another flies at the point of the formation. Geese in the rear honk to encourage those up front to speed up.

When a goose gets sick or wounded, two others drop out of formation and follow it down to help and provide protection. The helpers stay with the unhealthy member until it is either able to fly again or dies. They then launch out again with another passing flock or try to catch up with their own.

## No man is alone

"No single animal or plant is ever really alone. Neither are you nor I," wrote Douglas Wood from his cabin on Fawn Island, Minnesota.

John Donne once said famously, "No man is an island." But Douglas Wood said, "No island is an island. They are all connected under the surface."

He further adds, "Fawn island, with its circular form and trails, ancient greenstones and granites rooted deep in the mantle of the earth...is in many ways a loving Mandela--a symbol-- not of isolation but of connection to: the earth, the water, the sky."

"Our basic task as human beings ...is to demolish our own loneliness. To do this we need not only the help of other men and women, but the help of trees, flowers and animals," Wood tells us. "Without this help, this company, we are lost upon the earth no matter where we are, lost inside our own skins.... Who we are is *beings* sharing with *other beings* the mystery, terror and beauty of life." (italics added)

*Getting along with the enemy*

Jared Diamond tells us that the Dutch call the lands reclaimed from the sea in the Netherlands "polders." They began draining them 1,000 years ago, pumping out water that gradually seeps in, with windmills. Today they use steam, diesel, and electric pumps instead. The line starts with the pump farthest from the sea and pumps the water to the pumps that send it back into the river or ocean. The Dutch have an expression, "You have to get along with the enemy because he might be he one operating the neighboring pump in your polder." That is why the Dutch are so greatly aware of our environment. They have learned throughout history that we are all living in the same "polder".

Jared Diamond said: "We need to realize that there is no other planet we can turn to for help or export our problems. Instead we need to learn to live within our means, because we are the cause of our problems, we are the ones in control of them and we can choose or not choose to stop creating them and start solving them."

*Safety in groups*

"In no society worthy of the name do the members lack a sense of belonging and a need for acceptance," wrote Frans de Waal. "The ability and tendency to construct such validations, and to seek security within them, are products of natural selection found in members of species with better survival changes in a group than in solitude." Wall points out the advantages of group life in better foraging, defense and strength in numbers against completion.

"One obligatory behavior that every species has in common is the need to communicate," Roger Fouts wrote. "The ability to send and receive messages is crucial to the organization and survival of every animal society.... like birds and whales...the infant is born with a powerful drive to learn whatever system of communication is needs to socialize, mate or breed."

## *All living things depend on others to survive*

The apple-tree community is one example of Earth's many ecosystems. "The apple trees cannot make seeds or fruit if bees do not come to feed on the nectar of their blossoms," wrote Elaine Pascoe. "The earthworms eat leaves from the trees and improve the soil and the trees grow. The animals that eat apples scatter seeds so that new apple trees can sprout."

## *Animals: Important for planet survival*

"It has been claimed that the world could exist without animals, but that without plants, all life would soon disappear," write George W. Folkerts and Lucia Niemeyer.

"But there are many plants that would not last long without animals: animals being important in pollination, dispersal of seeds, the recycling process which keeps materials available in natural systems. Even so, green plants form the basis of the processes that support all life on this planet."

## *Curl up like a cat*

"Each day, I wake startled to be alive on a planet packed with so much life," wrote Diane Ackerman. "No ray of sunlight goes unused. Life homesteads every pore and crevice, including deep dark ocean trenches. We share our origins and future with the rest of life on earth. We need a healthy environment if we hope to stay healthy. But, nature also means comfort.

"Most days, I make time to play outside, usually in the garden or on a bike or taking a walk.... Surrounded by trees and sky, it's easier to feel a powerful sense of belonging to the pervasive mystery of nature, or being molded by unseen forces older than our daily concerns. Without that, life would feel flat as a postage stamp.

She recommends an activity she calls "spanieling". She finds a shaft of sunlight pouring though the window on a cold day and relishes the breath of sun on her skin. She curls up in the puddle of warmth it creates and naps the way a dog or cat would. "Steep yourself in nature," she concludes; "the world will wait."

*We have only so much time*

"We have only so much time," said Michio, a Japanese nature photographer in Alaska, as quoted in *The Blue Bear.* "I think this is what nature is always trying to tell us--that we are going to die someday, just like everything else in nature, and that's what makes us really want to *live.*"

# Chapter Two

# Mutual Respect

"O Lord, our Lord...
When I consider ...the work of your fingers...
what is man that you are mindful of him...?
You have made him ruler over the works of your hands;
You put everything under his feet:
all flocks and herds,
and the beasts of the field,
the birds of the air,
and the fish of the sea,
all that swim the paths of the seas.
Psalm 8: 1, 3a, 4a, 6-8 (*The Holy Bible*,
New International Version)

*Smart woodpecker*

In *Deathwatch*, Robb White wrote: "He had often wondered how a woodpecker could be so much smarter than a man. The Gila woodpecker knew better than to kill a giant saguaro: the bird, like man, left its mark on the giant cactus, but, unlike man, it never killed one....A man carving his initials in the skin of a saguaro, initials that will probably never been seen again by another man, can cause this giant...plant literally to bleed to death. And many men have done just that.

---

"The Gila woodpecker, on the other hand, knows when it is not safe to nest in the saguaro...

"It never injures the plant during rainy season, for the woodpecker depends on the saguaro.

"However, when a nest will do no damage, the woodpecker cuts a small, round hole through the tough side of the plant and works its way into the saguaro's...interior. Then the bird hollows out a place for the nest, and the plant soon coats the walls of the nest with a...plaster which not only keeps the moisture of the plant from running out and thus killing it, but keeps the nest dry and snug for baby Gila woodpeckers."

*Holy ground*

Phyllis Tickle told he following story that happened on a Tennessee farm where the family had moved so the children could learn about farm life. The children came into the house, and told her that Saint's calf was standing over the hill by the pond bawling. (Saint was a cow).

Tickle watched as all the cows came from the pasture and stood by the fence. Tickle knew they would not have come for people unless something was wrong. The family followed the calf, and the cows followed the people. They found Saint dead, and the cows moved back, knowing the people had found her. The family moved in a truck on which to load the dead cow to take it for burial, but then they noticed the bull coming across the pasture....

The family got into the truck bed, wondering if they needed to be concerned about their safety. The cows followed the bull. The bull ritually mounted the dead cow's carcass. Then the animal uttered a sound Phyllis had never heard from another animal, "a kind of call to the herd that was summons, explanation and completion." Then he simply lowered his head and moved. The cows paraded by and each sniffed the carcass and then moved back down the hill. The bull continued to watch as the family moved the carcass of the dead cow.

The family had witnessed what few farmers ever see.... They had been on holy ground and witnesses to the mysteries of another order. The next day the family went to church to observe The Feast of St. Michael and All saints--the one day of the year when all Christendom pays lip service to the invisible realities and unseen orders. Having been witnesses to another order, they were ready to recite from the *Book of Common Prayer:* "O Everlasting God, who hast ordained and constituted the ministries of angels and men in a wonderful order...."

## *We don't do well as gods*

Nature Writer Michael Katakis wrote: "We took the idea of dominion over the world and its creatures to mean ownership rather than stewardship, and then raised ourselves to a place we had not earned and were not suited for. We do not do well as gods. We, in fact, were never supposed to be God. We were supposed to be gardeners. As gods we lean more toward destruction than creation, cutting down and rooting up rather than cultivating."

Sigurd F. Olson wrote that the old Judeo-Christian philosophy was one of domination—ignoring the ancient ways of nature and molding it to our wishes—we must now look at the earth with recognition of our close relationship to all life.

"I try to practice a faith that teaches that God gave us dominion over the earth, but somehow, I think we've misunderstood this gift, its purpose," Ken Lamberton wrote. "Perhaps we need to change our definition of dominion as we've distanced ourselves from both God and nature. We are gardeners, not gods."

Elenthropomorphic thinking bridges a vital gap in nature. It helps to discredit the tightly held belief that aggressive dominance over species and nature makes sense. "For too long," said Douglas Chadwick, "we have fashioned a big moral loophole for ourselves so we can continue to exploit other beings without guilt or confusion."

"In the Judeo-Christian tradition, humans were given dominion over the earth and all living things," wrote Roger Fouts. "As a result, the early church fathers embraced the Great Chain of Being (designed by Aristotle) and crowned it with biblical man, a unique animal created in the image of God."

Nature Writer Michael Katakis wrote: "We took the idea of dominion over the world and its creatures to mean ownership rather than stewardship, and then raised ourselves to a place we had not earned and were not suited for. We do not do well as gods. We, in fact, were never supposed to be God. We were supposed to be gardeners. As gods we lean more toward destruction than creation, cutting down and rooting up rather than cultivating."

"In times like this it comes to me, the folly of what we're doing on the face of this world, behaving as if it were ours, utterly," wrote Barbara Kingsolver as she ponders the joy she experienced in nature. "And I wonder at the arrogance of the agenda we've inherited from our forebears."

"Water is the blood of a land," she wrote. It courses through the internal seams and passageways of a continent, cleansing and carrying nutrients to all its farthest reaches...." Yet, throughout our nation's history, she observed, we have participated in bloodletting: draining Southern marshes to raise crops; tapping aquifers and challenging rivers in the west to take care of the needs of ranches and farmers; damming rivers, strangling the natural flow of water; harnessing water to meet our needs of transportation, power and waste removal.

With regards to wetlands, she pointed out, Americans have looked on them as nuisances to be gotten rid of. The desecration of the Florida everglades is a prime example. Today, the US has drained more than half of its original wetlands.

"Earth is a water plane," wrote Linda Hogan. "It is a world

of salt oceans, cloud forests, undergoing springs and winding rivers.... Everywhere water travels, life follows."

## Swamp concert

Many years ago George Folkerts visited the Okeefenokee Swamp in South Georgia. He heard the frogs singing as they called for mates to come and reproduce. He had not heard this in many years. He said: "I fear that the frogs of the swamp are disappearing, as is the frog species around the world. Perhaps, I have heard the last deafening ten-voice serenade of the Okeefenokee. These beings are disappearing and some of the reasons are known, but some are so complex they are nearly indecipherable. We do know that the world is sick and in its stricken stage it is losing its tissues and organs. A world without frogs is a world without nightsong, a world without the announcement of its reproduction. While the euphony of the frog song remains, there is hope for the swamp and the planet."

## All life sacred

"Each living creature is worthy of our respect," wrote Davis LaChapelle. "We as humans have large, complex brains. This has led to the belief in the western world that we are superior to other animals. We have been able to dominate other animals and have been led to believe that all the world's riches and the other animals were created for our benefit. Darwin's theory of evolution brought more respect to animals, but the belief in humankind's superiority remained. Today's science is beginning to "prove" what most people have always intuitively known: that we humans are not the only, thinking, feeling beings on the planet." LaChapelle concluded: "This leads to a new respect for other animals who are fellow travelers with us on life's journey. We are beginning to see that each animal has a place and role in the world. Our attitudes are beginning to change. All lives become sacred and we become more careful with our care of them."

"As a result of the human population growth, hunting, environmental destruction, and pollution, other animal species have increasingly crowded out and their number depleted, often to the point of extinction," Jane Goodall wrote. "In the last hundred years, humans have been the cause of untold animal losses. The natural rate of extinction is about one species per one million species a year. About one new species per one million species is born each year."

"When the first European settlers walked into this drama they found mostly forests from the coast into present-day Indiana," wrote Kingsolver. "From the Wabash River westward, they encountered more grass than they'd ever imagined: 240 million acres.... The plow destroyed the grass, converting 240 million acres into cropland within 80 years."

*We are part of the animal kingdom*

"It is easier to share feelings of close connection with other animals when we recognize and appreciate that we are all part of the animal kingdom," Jane Goodall and Marc Bekoff wrote. "We can only tolerate so much alienation from our kin before the cycle of alienation reverses itself and reconnection is sought. Perhaps we humans view animals as having qualities we have lost and yearn for their presence, their pure emotion, their zest for life; let us rejoice that we are part of the animal kingdom."

*Animal feelings*

The French philosopher Rene Descartes, in the seventeenth century, took the position that animals had no feelings. If an animal cried out in pain when hit, for example, Descartes said it was reacting automatically rather than out of real pain. He felt humans were superior and disconnected from other animals.

But when Edward Tyson performed a dissection of chimpanzee in England in 1699, he saw a remarkable similarity to man's anatomy.

## *Health problems from polluted air*

In North America alone about 235 animal species are threatened by pollution, human encroachment on their habitat and aggressive harvesting practices, wrote Toby Hemenway. Around Puget Sound in Washington State, satellite images have shown a 40 percent loss of trees in the past two decades, which would have removed 35 million pounds of pollutants from the air. The United States spent about $100 billion on health problems related to air pollution during this period of time.

## *Population increase*

In October 1999, the world's population was declared to have reached the six billion mark, twice the population of 1960. It is estimated that the world's population will increase by three billion in the next 50 years. The current population is seven billion plus. Nearly 80 million people are added to the earth's population each year. That places pressure up0on our natural resources, wildlife habitats and the atmosphere.

The world's 50 poorest countries have the highest increase in births.

David Quammen wrote: "Biologists call it an outbreak when certain types of animals have an explosive increase over a relatively short period of time. We are familiar with the 17-year plague of locusts, for example. He quoted Entomologist Alan A. Berryman who wrote: "From the ecological point of view...the most serious outbreak on the planet earth is that of the species Homo sapiens," referring to the fact that the human population has increased by more than double within only the last century.

Major species extinction

There have been five major species extinctions since life evolved on the planet. Scientists estimate the current species extinction rate to be between 40 to 1,000 times the background rate of extinction. We are living through another major species extinction. One in eight plants worldwide in under threat. Over half the primates are in danger. Since 1900, 123 freshwater species of marine life have disappeared. The cause of the sixth extinction is clear: we are our own enemy. Humans have introduced changes into the ecosystem that are responsible for launching of a possible sixth extinction event. The die off has not yet reached the level of a major extinction, but left unchecked, current patterns will almost assuredly produce one.

# Chapter Three

# Nature's Effect on people

Flowers appear on the earth;
the season of singing has come,
the cooing of doves
is heard in our land.
The fig tree forms its early fruit;
the blossoming vines spread their fragrance.
(Song of Songs: 2:12-13, *The Holy Bible*,
New International Version)

## Surviving Prison through Nature

Ken Lamberton, a high school science teacher in Arizona, was married with two children and a third on the way. He became obsessed with a former 14-year-old student, ran away with her and was sentenced to 12 years in prison. Nature kept him sane while he was there, teaching science to fellow prisoners. He wrote a book about his prison experiences entitled *Wilderness and Razor Wire*, illustrating it with his own drawings.

This is his story: "My wilderness is a limited geographical area, not one bound by mountains, rivers or oceans, but by chain link fence and razor wire. My wilderness is a prison. All the same it is a wilderness with its nuances of seasonal change, summer droughts and winter freezes, rain, dust, and wind; with its microcosms of water, of weeds, trees, birds and insects. Nature is here as much as it is in any national park or forest or monument, but some people hardly notice nature here."

Lamberton talked about prison life and how difficult it is to connect with nature in such a place, yet some prisoners do: " It would be a simple matter to wake up each morning a body on a mattress that moves slowly through another pointless day, a body at meals, a body in front of the television, a body that lives without participating in life. It is easy to lack emotions, perception. What's difficult--but most rewarding--is to sense wilderness in this place. The men whose cells are near a swallow's nest continue to impress me with their sensitivity for the birds. They monitor them year after year, counting the eggs, and marking off the days to hatching and fledgling."

The prison grounds became an artificial wetland that enhanced wild life. "Because of the sewage treatment plant being taxed, the Arizona Department of Corrections changed how it dealt with its wastewater at the Tucson Complex. Reclaiming this water, prison grounds became an artificial wetland kept green and wet by a new effluent irrigation system, creating an island that attracts swallows," Lamberton said.

"The prison is overcrowded, and twenty-one hundred flushing toilets has done more than settle the dust under a mat of vegetation; it has turned the bleak place into a wildlife island and a rest stop and refuge for birds."

The prison administrators decided that the trees in the visitation area where families and prisoners could have picnics together provided a security problem. They thought the men could possibly climb the trees and escape over the fence, so they cut down the trees and closed the area. Lambert had a strong emotional response. "I walk past a picket line to treeless trunks and see muscular arms with chopped off hands reaching upward in some kind of plea of the maimed and dying. I'm irrational because I value something here. I've risked love. My emotional response is the evidence. The trees did more than dissolve the gray wall and razor wire, purifying the very cast of this prison. They were more than analgesic to numb my punishment, the fear and depression. They were a living point of reference that gave me a sense of direction--physically and emotionally. The trees helped me to keep a bearing on how I felt about my family. They connected me to reality beyond prison.

"I try to practice a faith that teaches that God gave us dominion over the earth, but somehow, I think we've misunderstood this gift, its purpose." He concluded: "Perhaps we need to change our definition of dominion as we've distanced ourselves from both God and nature. We are gardeners, not gods."

*Life is circular*

At age 17, Eustace Conway left his comfortable suburban home to move into the Appalachian Mountains in North Carolina in 1977. He has lived in a teepee he designed on the thousand acres he owns, after accumulating that total acreage piece by piece. He calls his home Turtle Island, so named for the creationist legend of Native Americans of the turtle who carries the weight of the entire earth on his back.

Conway considers his world as the ultimate teaching facility, a university in the raw. After years of studying primitive societies and after countless experiences of personal transformation within the wilderness, Eustace has formed a mighty dogma. He feels that modern America can begin to reverse its inherent corruption and greed and malaise by feeling the rapture that comes from face-to-face encounters with what he call "the high art and godliness of nature."

Conway believes that we as Americans are constantly striving for convenience and replacing our natural beauty with a safe but completely faux environment. He thinks this is why we are an increasingly depressed and anxious people. He said, "I live in nature, where everything is connected, circular...the seasons are circular. The planet is circular and so is its passage around the sun. The course of water over the earth is circular...coming from the sky passing around the earth and evaporating back up to the sky again. The life cycles of plants and animals are circular." He concludes: "People say that I don't live in the real world, but it's modern Americans who live in a fake world, because they've stepped outside the natural circle of life."

When Conway looks around our nation, he sees a people who have lost that vital connection with nature, therefore the nation is in danger of losing its humanity. He sees a chilling sight—people so greatly removed from the rhythms of nature that we march through our lives as mere sleepwalkers. But he believes that we can get our humanity back. We can do that by being "mindful of every nuance of our natural world...: that we are each given only one dazzling moment of life here on Earth, and we must stand before that reality both humbled and elevated, subject to every law of our universe and grateful for our brief...participation within it."

Conway observed that most people complain about the weather when it interferes with what they want to do that day. He wrote in his journal that "there is no such thing as a 'bad' day in nature. You can't stand in judgment of nature like that because she always does what she needs to do."

*Everything important in a natural world*

Dorothy Gilman, a successful novelist, found herself divorced at 40. She relocated to Nova Scotia where she felt traumatized by a long list of things to do. "Until one day something stirred inside me, and I looked out at the harbor and the ocean and the sun slanting through the windows, and I kept walking through the door and out in to the soft fragrance of an October morn," she wrote. On the beach she laughed out loud, and laughing in the sun, she felt the rigidities inside her let go and it was a beginning.

She looked at the incredibly luminous quality to the light there: the sun reached the earth without smog, glancing off rocks and water, turning the sky a vivid blue. The water that reflected it was a sapphire or cobalt and flittered under the sun until it flooded her senses.

Gilman turned into the path leading to the beach, discarding her dew-drenched shoes and continued down the path barefooted. "Each rock I passed held a drop of dew in its hollow center that looked--as the sun set it afire--like a diamond dropped there during the night. The grass was rough as rattan on my feet, and wet. When I reached the shore my feet ached with cold, and I climbed up on a rock to warm them before I ventured on the beach." The tide was low, and when it retreated, it had left water and sea life behind it in small hollows and crevices. She found periwinkles clinging to the rocks, minnows in small ponds, empty clam and mussel shells, and long brittle ropes of kelp. She smelled a thick fragrance of salt in the air and of rich decaying muck. When she turned to go back, something strange had happened.

The sun, not high enough yet in the sky to flood the shore with light, was just illuminating a long row of rocks along the shore. Each rock was densely covered with seaweed, and in this juxtaposition--of soft golden light and long slanted shadow--the rocks looked like human heads in a row staring primly out to sea…"a line of gossipy ladies nodding in the sun," she wrote And standing there laughing on the beach in the morning sun, Gilman felt the rigidities inside her release as an iron band that holds a barrel together by its staves. Putting on her shoes, she hurried up the hill to breakfast.

But it was a beginning. The new kind of world she was inhabiting began to have a realness for her that no other ever had. She discovered that in a small, more natural world, there is space for relationship and for contact. Everything became important. She and her eight tomato plants went through crisis after crisis the first year. In October, when she dug them out of the soil to add to the compost file, she felt as if she were ending a long and intimate friendship, and there were tears in her eyes. Where she lived, there were no garden supply houses to sell her organic materials wrapped in shiny sealed bags.

When Gilman's older son Christopher came for several weeks' vacation in August, the two spent a day making forays into the woods for pine needles and rich humus, and then to the beach for muck, which they mixed with sawdust and wood chips from the lumberyard in town. All of these materials fed the earth, and the earth fed the vegetables. Everything had its use. When she built a wood fire for warmth, she became aware that the wood had reached her by a long process. She had first met it when it was dumped in her yard in the spring, after which she laboriously stacked the three cords piece by piece in the sun for seasoning; and then in the fall, she carted and moved it--piece by piece--to the barn for the winter. "My neighbor...said there is warm heat and cold heat; I only understood what he meant after adding wood stoves to my life," she wrote.

Gilman also harvested wild plants, making teas and drinking them individually or mixing them with juices, and making salads or cooking the plants. It surprised her to recognize that, except for paying her sons' college tuitions, she had lived on less than $3,000 for the year--without trying to. "Nature had supplied the abundance and most of my recreation as well," she recorded. One day she treated an old stubborn wound: washing dishes had delayed the healing of a cut finger. She rubbed a dried comfrey leaf into powder that she sprinkled onto a wet bandage and wrapped it around the finger. Three nights later she found herself noticing a white scar on a tanned finger, wondering where it came from. Amazed, she realized this was all that was left of her stubborn, angry red cut. She wondered: "Can anyone rationally suggest there is no order to the universe when there are such small potent miracles as herbs abroad?"

Gilman concluded that the real seasons of the year are not

marked by the calendar, but in the completion of that cycle there was a deep sense of rhythm, of ebb and flow, a feeling of everything dovetailing and fitting together such as she had never experienced before. As a result, she came to see that society contrives to rob people of a friendship with the earth and its seasons. "Or perhaps it was even simpler than this; perhaps it was what my neighbor said when she first viewed the great sweep of harbor and sky from my window: 'You must feel very close to God here'. "

Her son Jonathan visited her in February. When the pipes froze one day, he marveled at how calm she was, remembering how greatly upset she would have become three years earlier in New Jersey.

## Creating paths

"I love to create paths," wrote Lisa Peck. "When I was a young girl, growing up in a truly small, central New York town, I convinced my sister and some of our friends to bring rakes, shovels and any other helpful garden tools out to a forest near our home. We gathered them all up and walked along the edge of the neighbors' cornfield for about a half a mile or so until we reached the entrance to the forest."

The girls discussed their project at great length as to where it might lead and what forms of entertainment they would have along the way. The project could lead to a fort, one child would suggest. Another would add that they needed to go straight down the hill with it so they would have a running place. They would build a home for toads or even snakes; they'd wind their path down by the swinging vines, and they'd be sure to head it back up the hill toward the large fallen tree where they could sit and have lunch.

"Truth being told," Peck continued, "our imaginations did not match the effort any of them was willing to put forth." The girls started working, under her insistent supervision, but the path wasn't looking the way any of them had imagined it would, and it was a slow process. After a fair amount of effort, one by one, their motivation dissolved, and they decided to go hunt for salamanders and the big white fungus that they loved to scratch words or pictures on with sturdy sticks.

Many years later, during her 20's, Peck moved to a little house that bordered on a couple of acres of woodland. They began another path project. This time, she worked alone and kept a realistic imagine in mind. "It was great," she recalls. "The path led by an apple tree that blossomed heavenly in spring and through a very pretty shade area where she planted tulips. The path continued winding down toward a small pond. She would walk down it in the morning with her first cup of coffee and listen for the beaver to slap its' wide, flat tail as she approached. Sometimes she would see him retreating through the water to the other side of the pond.

During her 30's, she moved yet again with a friend who had recently bought a farmhouse with a very large yard that bordered on a wooded lot. Together, as the two explored, they discovered that, at some distant point in the past, someone had been maintaining a path along the woods edge and into the woods. "We followed it as best we could, losing it at times and finding it again," she sighs. "It led to a small wooden bridge that crossed an equally small creek. It was lovely."

The two agreed that Peck would clear it once again so they would have a walkable path through the woods. She set to the task immediately, spending hours each day, clipping and pruning small trees and moving rocks and fallen debris. She planted flowers and placed a birdhouse on the path and groomed it into a beautiful walking area. Often, in the morning, she would get her cup of coffee and stroll down the path, making mental notes of what else could be done to improve it. She would also take evening walks down the path, silently admiring her work.

One evening, as she started out on the path, she noticed that the birds were chirping especially loudly. "They were making an unusually persistent racket, chirping and giving me the distinct feeling that something was not right." Somewhat perplexed, she continued on and walked the path farther into the woods, down to the creek and back to the starting point. Again, as I returned to the beginning of the path, the birds—lots of them—were chirping loudly, more so than usual." She stopped. Their sounds were alarm, close to panic. At that point, Peck looked down and saw a baby bird in the middle of the path. It had barely any feathers, and upon closer examination, she noted that it was definitely dead. "I was astonished," she recalls.

She stepped over the bird and went to retrieve something to bury it with. The birds in the trees continued their loud squawking. She returned with a shovel and placed the point on the ground beside the bird and pushed down with her foot. She scooped the dirt and the bird into the shovel and lifted it up. With one motion, she flipped the whole pile upside down into the earth, effectively burying it.

The birds immediately stopped all their noise. Every single bird was silent. "I was amazed," she said. Moments before, the sounds were noisily incessant, and now nothing—not one lone voice. "After my amazement subsided somewhat, I felt an overwhelming sense of gratitude, which I attributed to the now silent creatures in the trees."

## No wild land is ever silent

"The first thing you notice about the desert is light. It is such a bright light that washes out everything," Bruce Feiler wrote of his response to the Sinai desert. "The dessert may be defined as the absence of rain, but a water color painting of the place would have far more water than color." The second thing he noticed was space. The panorama was overwhelming. Two eyes were not enough to take in the scene and two arms were not enough to embrace it; and the Sinai would diminish any crowd. The last thing one would notice was the noise. In this part of preparing for the journey, Feiler steeled himself for the silence. But he was amazed by the din…the wind whining through the mountains, the sand hitting against his face, the rocks crunching under his feet. No wild land is ever really silent, he noticed. The dessert may be empty, but it's the least quiet place he had ever been…and the most alluring. "The Sinai, in particular--compels a certain clarity," he wrote. "Come with a vague sense of identity and leave with a deeper sense of self. If God knew this, as the Bible suggests, he may indeed have known everything."

Feiler interviewed Israel Hershkovitz, a professor of anatomy and anthropology at Tel Aviv University, who said; "It makes sense to me that the desert is where most of the great religions of the world were born. More than any other place, it gives you time for thinking about spiritual things. I know when you go to certain places you become a better person…." He noted that when he goes into the desert he becomes a better person.

"By its (the desert's) sheer demands—thirst, hunger, misery— it asks a simple question: 'What is in your heart?' Or, put another way, 'In what do you believe?'" Feiler continued.

"This act of reconnecting with the past…is largely what I was undergoing on my trip through the desert…. I was wriggling free from the firm grip of modern life and inching toward something else, something more instinctive and untaught." He found himself breaking away from modes of thought he had used since he was a teenager—reason, skepticism, logic, learning—and moving toward modes of relating to the world—emotion, intuition, trust—that he probably hadn't relied on much since he was a child. In doing so, he felt himself slide further away from the rigid, controlled person he was at the beginning of this process. He was…to use the local vernacular…more of a roll-out carpet. He was conforming to the land.

*Nature's "rules"*

Why do natural sites always look beautiful and stay nearly disease free without human care while gardens require a lot of work? The answer is simple: *Gardeners ignore nature's rules.*

"Nature always stacks functions, because any living thing represents a big investment in matter and energy, two things that nature husbands with immense stinginess," wrote Toby Hemenway. "She is supreme at getting the most bang for her buck tying into a lot of cycles to maximize the return: A simple compost pile is multifunctional as it disposes of waste, create humus, boosts soil life, and even offers the gardener exercise by spreading it. The concept of stacking functions has two halves: the first is that each element of a design or plant structure should do more than one job."

The author's grapevine, for example, shades the deck, cools the house, provides food, mulch, and propagation stock, and helps beautify a water tank. The second principal is that each job to be done in a design should always have a backup. He believes that an ugly landscape cramps the soul while a beautiful one invites, relaxes and heals the viewer. "No human designed an Alpine meadow, or a tropical forest, or a creek side grotto, yet these wild landscapes are never ugly. They follow a natural order that seems to ensure beauty. Nothing in nature stands alone and disconnected. No one brings fertilizer into a forest or carries its waste to the dump. The forest takes care of all of that internally, producing fertility and recycling litter and debris. Sunlight powers do virtually all the work."

*Treasure winter's wonders*

"I look forward to the finish of the holiday hustle and the quiet of January and February, when even the whistling teakettle sounds rich, comfortable, not shrill as it does in hotter months," wrote Susan Straight. These months allow us to think and dream while our blood runs a bit more slowly, and we don't worry yet about what comes next, she comments.

She urges us to see the quiet. "We so often look down—at our phones or our bills or our steering wheels," she said. "Look skyward instead, at the landscape of winter."

*Nature: a patient teacher*

"The wilderness exerts enormous influence on a man alone freshly arrived from civilization," wrote R.D. Lawrence. "Some cannot take solitude, the absence of comfort. They don't last, but there are others who go too far the other way, becoming misanthropes. But between the two are the ones to who nature acts as a catalyst. They began to form new values, and to realize that nature is an endlessly patient teacher. This is how the wilderness affected me."

Lawrence, born in Spain of English parents, had his adolescence cut short by service in both the Spanish Civil War and World War II. Those experiences left him profoundly affected, and he developed an armor against emotion. "Yukon (his part-wolf dog) ended that," he wrote. "He made me feel the need for a being other than myself. When we were together, I found peace with nature. Nature was and is a healing agent for me."

*Wait and hope*

Reflecting on the tragedies of the shootings at the Columbine High School; the attacks of 9/11, the loss of seven astronauts on the Columbia and the war in Iraq, the Rev. Edwin Chase compared our grief and loss that seeps into our homes with the relentless dust of the Dust Bowl of the 1930s. "Despite every effort the people could not keep the wind driven dust out of their homes. I wonder what folks do after a sandstorm?

After thinking about it, I would suggest three things: pray, plant something and wait." He continued, "Eventually the wind subsides and the dust settles, but before you begin you must realize that reclaiming the land after as storm doesn't happen over night. It takes time. Every prayer is like a seed planted; some fall by the wayside; some are trampled; but we plant them by faith that some will sprout and some day they will make a difference in the landscapes of our lives. Next, actually plant something is the ground. A tree…a plant. If it dies, just plant another one."

Chase wrote about Willam A, Fickling Sr. of Macon, Georgia, who inspired an entire community to plant the city in Yoshino Cherry trees. Now, every spring, the city is resplendent with pink cherry blossoms that transform the landscape. Some trees die, so city employees plant new ones.

"Finally," Chase suggested, "plant something new in someone's life. Plant lots of seeds. Some fall by the way side; some are trampled; but some will sprout and make a difference in the landscape of our world. Then wait with hope."

*Play in the dirt again*

Gardening isn't just a fun way to beautify your garden and product fruits and vegetables. It can also bring health benefits. It can lower your blood pressure and leave you with a healthier heart.

We live in a stressful world which can take its toll on the heart. It can be difficult to find the time to relax and escape from the pressures of the world. In the garden, this becomes much easier. As people step away from every day life and turn to nature, they will find peace and relax. Working in a garden also gives great exercise without having to go a gym. Also, gardeners have healthier choices of food available. A combination of reducing stress, exercising more and eating healthier can lead to reduced blood pressure.

The American Horticulture Therapy Association believes that

horticulture therapy is a time proven practice for both physical and mental illnesses. The therapeutic benefits of peaceful garden environments have been understood since ancient times. Dr. Benjamin Rush, a signer of the Declaration of Independence and considered to be "Father of American Psychiatry" reported that garden settings held curative effects for people with mental illness.

Rehabilitative care of hospitalized war veterans in the 40's and 50's greatly expanded the practice of horticulture therapy. Today it is recognized as a practical and viable treatment with wide-ranging benefits for people in therapeutic, vocational and wellness programs.

Horticulture therapy is now taught and practiced throughout the world in a rich diversity of settings and cultures.

The members of this organization are seeing a tremendous increase in interest in horticulture therapy, partly because people are eager about the quality of life as the population ages and how to make gardening accessible for everyone.

They advocate gardening not just for the aging, but for children with autism, youth in prisons and young people with mental illness. The physically and developmentally disabled benefit greatly because gardening so well suits their needs.

For the patients being treated at the Wesley Woods Center of Emory Health Care, Decatur, GA, the words "Play in the dirt again" mean more than an advertising slogan, thanks to the geriatric hospital's horticultural therapy program.

Headed by Kirk Hines, horticultural therapist, and founded in 19993, the HTP is a component of the hospital's rehabilitation services department. The program allows patients to enjoy gardens and a greenhouse as well as attend small classes where they get their hands dirty and enjoy gardening. "As people work toward recovery, it's important to do things that are active but relaxing," Hines explained. "Working with plants helps them relax and reduces blood flow pressure and reduces pain levels."

Even though insurance doesn't cover horticultural therapy as it does other types of physical and occupational therapy, Emory offers it because it is so helpful to the patients.
Gardening benefits Alzheimer's' patients. Physical as well as visual access to nature helps people recover from illness quicker and reduces stress and lowers blood pressure. Spending time outside helps people maintain circadian rhythms (the sleep/wake cycle). Elements of a garden help a person stay connected to the world around them through sights, sounds, fragrances and touch. Nature can reduce anxiety, blood pressure, pain, and stress symptoms and improve sleep patterns. The sick and elderly who are able to view trees and sky recover faster than those staring at brick walls.

Gardening is familiar territory to Alzheimer's' patients and gives them a sense of still being able to do something. It also stimulates memory.

At Emory's University's Wesley Wood Geriatric Center, gardening helps elderly stroke victims recover motor skills and motivates he depressed with a daily routine. At the Shepard Center in Atlanta, patients with brain and spinal cord injuries build strength and endurance by using adapted cuffs for holding tools to tend several gardens. At the DeKalb Services Center, also in Atlanta, the mentally and in some cases physically disabled don't just help master gardeners maintain a big vegetable garden, they also deliver the produce to charities served by a local food drive called "plant a row for the hungry."

Osteoporosis, a bone disease that robs its victims of bone density and strength, can cause chronic pain, permanent disability and worst. It costs the United States an estimated $15 billion a year. Gardening is one of the best forms of physical exercise for increasing bone density.

In a study of 3,000+ older women, University of Arkansas researchers found that women involved in yard work and other types of gardening exercises had lower rates of osteoporosis than joggers, swimmers and those who did aerobics.

That likely has to do with the fact that gardening is sort of like weight training: gardeners just pull weeds; dig holes; carry heavy loads of soil; and compost; and do other forms of weight bearing activities that ward off osteoporosis.

A few miles away in Atlanta at the Skyland Trail Health and Education Center, adults with mental illness have helped cultivate extensive gardens, and in doing so have developed self-esteem. For clients who have not had a lot of success in life, growing a plant helps to connect with them in a way that leads to socialization, and if they master something, they can go on to teach someone else. Gardening is accessible and nonthreatening and doesn't have to cost a lot.

## Living by the seasons

In my work as a psychotherapist, I often have women clients who are stressed, depressed and anxious. Some are having panic attacks. A common characteristic among these women is the fact that they are pushing themselves to live at "full throttle" all of the time. One woman, in her 50's who desires to write, has even managed to create a room in her home that's a retreat where she could pray, meditate, and write. But she can never go into the room to do those desired activities. "There's always something I need to do," she said.

I point out to these women that Nature has four seasons and that each is necessary for its complete work to be accomplished. During winter, Nature sleeps. It's not productive. Winter is essential for spring to happen, the time when new life bursts forth. Spring is necessary for summer to happen, when plants produce at high peak. Then in autumn, Nature slows down, taking a rest that leads to winter.

In our culture, we expect people to live in summer all year

round, to produce at high speed. We hear a lot of SHOULD messages: *You should stay busy all of the time.* The result is that people stay exhausted and have little joy in life.

When I lived in the Caribbean for 12 years, I developed a siesta habit. Even though I've been back in the States for many years, I continue that habit. Once, my family visited one of my sisters (where I took my daily nap). One day she said, "You waste a lot of time by taking naps." That accusation contained a strong SHOULD message, that I should work all of the time.

When we lived in Santo Domingo (during the final four-year term of our Caribbean stay), I had a maid who served dinner to the family, therefore it was possible for me to be absent then. I developed a plan: each Monday afternoon, I would visit the air conditioned United States Embassy library for a few hours to read and write. I never went there once. I couldn't give myself permission to take that time to enrich and renew myself. (But I did take daily naps!)

My friend, Darlene, in her 70's, retired a few months ago. She stays involved with her husband, grown children and grandchildren. "People keep asking me 'What are you DOING?' " Darlene told me. "And I tell them, 'Only what I *want* to do.' "

*America's quietest place*

The Hoh Rain Forest in Washington's Olympic National Park is the quietest place in America. Robert Earle Howells, who visited there, said that "quiet is the world as it was before we introduced artificial noise.

…"noise works insidiously, raising our blood pressure and heart rate, and causing hormonal changes with potentially far-reaching consequences, including anxiety, stress, nervousness, nausea, headaches, sexual impotence, mood swings and neuroses," Howells wrote. "Noise has even been linked to a small increase in cardiovascular disease. The World Health Organization estimates that in Western Europe, at least a million healthy life years are lost annually due to traffic-related noise alone."

Kurt Fristrup, PhD, national Park Service senior scientist and sound specialist, says the loss of quiet is: "literally a loss of awareness." Quiet, he claims, is tragically disappearing, and most of us aren't noticing.

"Quiet rarely means silent,"said Gordon Hempton, an acoustic ecologist who specializes in recordings of nature; he considers it to be an absence of human-generated noise.

"Biologists recognize that for animals, quiet is critical," wrote Howells. "The loss of natural quiet would be a catastrophe for the human soul."

Dr. Joyce Brothers wrote: "Scientists have found that being in touch with nature helps human beings. Noise is known to increase anxiety and stress and to cause tempers to explode."

*The best excuses for going outdoors*

"Stepping outside can help anyone feel better instantly," wrote Cristian Tudino "But it turns out that the perks of greener environs reach far beyond your mood: in their book, *Your Brain on Nature*, Eva Selhub, MD, and naturopath Alan Logan explore the incredible physiological effects of being outside. Here are five research-backed ways to experience nature's healing touch.

*Reap while you sow.* Norwegian researchers discovered that gardening provides an ideal distraction from the rumination that fuels depression.

*Exercise in the open air.* One study found that people who walked outdoors moved at a faster pace, perceived less exertion, and experienced more positive emotions than those who walked on an indoor treadmill. A Scotland study showed that people who walked through rural areas viewed their to-do lists as more manageable than those who walked on city streets.

*Notice the scenery.* Just looking at a natural scene causes people to have a positive outlook and emotional stability and to recall happy memories.

*Evaporate depression.* Negative ions, particles that are plentiful near waterfalls, breaking waves and river rapids—can act as natural antidepressants.

*Walk in the woods.* The Japanese say that *shinrin-yoku,* or "forest bathing," does wonderful things for the body. In one study, women who spent two to four hours in the woods on two consecutive days experienced a nearly 50 percent increase in the activity of cancer fighting white blood cells.

## Connecting to trees

"I always felt connected to the trees in Chicago," wrote Sandra Cisneros, best-selling author. "I was one of those children who felt more at home sitting in a tree reading a book than with another child. I felt, when I was a child, that trees could talk, and I understood what they could say. I could talk to the trees. And because of their age and wisdom, they told me to persevere, to "keep, keep, keep." They were also sympathetic and kind and friendly in a way that human beings were not; and they laughed and nodded a lot. But most of all, their lesson was one of patience."

She still feels that she's happiest when she's in her back yard underneath the trees looking out at the river. It brings her back to when she was a little girl, back to that solitude and that place. It makes her feel like creating. It takes her back to the place of the imagination.

"One of the big pleasures of my life is meditating in my back yard and watching the white cranes, because my friend from Oklahoma told me that those cranes are sacred to the Indians," she continued. "They say that when you see one, you're supposed to say a prayer, because they take your prayer to heaven. And to me that's the most wonderful image to think of. Whenever I see them, I say a prayer."

The first time she saw one she was so startled—she thought it was a man's business shirt that had flown off the clothesline! Then she realized it was a bird, but she'd never seen anything like that. "I always feel there's something mystical about the cranes coming," she mused.

"I feel as if my house is this boat and I'm docked in this little green sea," she concluded. "I don't have to leave the confines of my property to feel close to nature."

### Gardening feels good

"There's this plain, simple fact: Gardening just feels good," maintained Lee May. "It is a wonderful way to contemplate life's gifts. And as we age, we savor more, having developed greater appreciation for earthly pleasures as well as for mortality.

"This is quite unlike our youthful days, when we knew we'd live forever."

### Gardeners are good people

"Gardeners are fond of saying, rightly, that you almost never find a plant lover who is a bad person," wrote May. "I've always believed that. There's something about connecting with the soil that helps make connections with people, something that makes you want to treat them right."

### Gardening gives people a sense of pride

"Officials from the Atlanta Housing Authority, county extension services and the Atlanta Urban Gardening Program cite rising interest in gardening among residents of the city's 45 public-housing sites, which are home to some 34,000 residents," wrote May. "Among the results, experts say, are a heightened sense of community, relief of stress and increased self-esteem."

"Garden clubs are springing up in many of the complexes," said Cynthia Hoke, spokeswoman for the housing authority, adding that growing food and flowers "gives people a sense of pride." Robert Brannen, a Fulton County extension agent for 15 years, said, "Some people say the gardens reduce crime because when you have a community garden, people keep an eye on it."

## Gardening gives children respect for the earth

"Every gardening child I've ever known has had a healthy respect for the earth, carrying about what belongs on it—and what doesn't." wrote May. "No trash. I cannot imagine a child gardener tossing a candy wrapper into somebody's yard."

He wrote about two sisters, Karen and Vicky, who garden as time allows. During a drive, Karen saw some walkers throw down trash, prompting Vicky to say that such behavior "makes the earth sick."

Later, when Karen saw someone throwing trash from a car, she said, "They are bad, and they need to go to time-out."

May commented: "We need more like those girls. Before the sickness overcomes us."

## Gardening Heals

May recalled when he put in his first water feature, a little pond. He dug the hole one Sunday, when he was fighting the flu. "In sad shape, I walked out and looked at the little pond, knowing I couldn't dig out the hard, red clay in the condition my condition was in," he wrote. He took his pick and shovel from the shed and poked a shallow hole or two—"Just to get a feel for the project. For later." Next thing he knew, he had dug a pond some two feet deep. He continued, putting a layer of sand in the hole, leveling the molded pond as he filled it with water.

When it was all over, and the goldfish were swimming happily, he discovered that the flu was gone; it was a miracle, one repeated over and over for anyone who puts holes in the dirt—for water or plant. "Gardening heals," he concluded.

# Chapter Four

# What Animals Teach Us About Family Life

"But ask the animals, and they will teach you,
or the birds of the air, and they will tell you;
or speak to the earth, and it will teach you,
or let the fish of the sea inform you."
Job 12:7, 8 (*The Holy Bible*, New International Version)

*Birds learn to sing from their fathers*

"Singing is the key to success for most male songbirds in two of the most important things they will do in their lives—attract a male and hold on to a territory. So it is vital that they quickly learn the songs specific to their species," wrote Charles Seabrook, nature writer.

"To do so, the young birds must spend much time practicing and honing their singing skills." For most songbirds, he told us, singing doesn't come naturally. They must learn to sing, similar to the human babies learn to talk by hearing and observing adults, especially their parents. He names some exceptions that inherit all the genetic instructions they need to sing the appropriate song.

"Among songbirds who learn to sing, the father is a key model. Since the males are the only ones that sing in most songbird species, the young birds must strive to sound like their fathers to be successful in life," he continued Their fathers were the birds who sang loudly and sweetly during the nesting season in spring.

In late July, people are hearing the recently fledged sons as they practice to reach perfection. As such, most of the birds song being heard at that time may be a bit raspy and hesitant—not the smooth, mellifluous tunes heard from the adults in the spring. The young may practice for hours on end for weeks in a row until they can sing like their fathers.

Some birds, Seabrook said, will learn only one or two songs. Others, such as the mockingbird and the catbird, may learn dozens of tunes. "But the champion singer, the brown thrasher—Georgia's state bird—may acquire as many as 2,000 songs during its lifetime."

It is heartbreaking to teenage boys and young men on television who have committed crimes who are predominantly accompanied by their mothers. The fathers abandoned the families. What songs did those males learn from their fathers?

*Animals defend their young*

"It is in defense of their young that animals display the most amazing disregard for their personal safety," wrote Alexander Skutch. An animal will attack a larger animal or a man to try and protect their offspring. "Courage in defense of home and young is only one of the forms that parental devotion takes. It reveals itself even more so in the day to day tasks of caring for them. Animal and birdwatchers have watched them feed their nestlings or young even when they themselves are hungry. Mammals carry their young until they grow large and heavy and become a burden to carry. Certain animal are capable to form strong personal attachments, usually to their own species, but sometimes to other species as well; sometimes it is difficult to see what or if any material advantage that the animal gains from this companionship."

*Elephants bond as families*

Dr. Daphne Sheldrick had worked with elephants for 50 years at the time of this writing. She now works at the David Sheldrick Wildlife Trust, an orphanage she founded on the outskirts of Nairobi, Kenya. She said: "Due to the loss of habit and hunting of tusks for ivory. African elephants have lost much of their habitat, resulting in many orphaned elephants. The elephants have lost the wisdom of their elders and this has a profound effect on their lives. When a tiny calf is deprived of its family, it has lost that which is most important in a life that should span three score years and ten--the family. A highly social being, an elephant's perception of the world, like a child's, is molded in youth by those who surround it.

Young elephants grow up in a warm maternal atmosphere. "No other species on earth build their lives so tightly around their immediate and extended family members than elephants, not even humans," she continued. "Their reality is shaped by their childhood experiences in the herd. African elephants are in competition with a swiftly growing number of humans for every resource and space is a premium."

Elephants are self-aware and live empathetically; the experiences of others become their own. Elephants can communicate with others over long distances.

*Bears and orangutans need someone to teach them*

"Black bears are extremely good mothers, and only an imminent threat to their own lives will make them abandon their young," wrote Robert Caputo. "Bears are sensitive, intelligent and emotional creatures that need more than food. They need security, affection and someone to teach them. "

Barbara Harrison, in her book *Orangutan,* said: "All orangutans will, in the baby stage, develop an emotional attachment to anyone who cares for them, however poorly. Depending on their care they will develop certain characteristics: fear, if they are treated badly; extreme naughtiness if they are allowed to do as they please; disinterest and immobility if they are left in a confined space with nothing to arouse their curiosity and emotions. All these conditions can lead to sickness and even death in extreme cases."

*Male animals make good fathers*

Jeffery Moussaieff Masson wrote *The Emperor's Embrace: Reflections on Animals Families and Fatherhood* when he became convinced that animals feel the same emotions as people. Throughout human history, Masson observed, fathers have had minimal interaction with their children based on biological grounds and that male animals don't do that. He contended that this is incorrect, studying the emperor penguin for evidence. These fathers hold the eggs under their bellies on their feet barely moving or eating through the unbearable winter of four-and-a-half months until their mates returns from their time at sea.

Masson reported that male wolves make good fathers after choosing a mate (many times for life); they father their young alone; but wolves raise their young to eventually leave the den… when humans fail to do this, their children fail to achieve emotional maturity, economic independence, and other skills required to live a successful life. Mason believed that wolves are superior to other animals when it comes to emotions. He stated that: "it is a rare instance when a male animal kills its own child. That kind of infanticide seems to be reserved for humans alone…."

Masson observed other animals be good fathers to their young and he believes that instinct is also built into humans. He also thought that we have harmful prejudices among which is the mistaken idea in the popular imagination that no other no other animal is a good father since men are animals.

He said, "It is only natural to disappear after copulation. Male remoteness is sanctioned by our civilization, it is even expected...this goes contrary to nature. Children need from us warmth, comfort, protection, food, shelter, clothing, education, and medical attention," he wrote. "Prolonged play with the child is good for the father and child and gives the mother a break. We also evolved to travel with our children. No other society posts signs that an establishment is *For Adults Only*. In every other society, children follow their parents to work as soon as they are old enough."

Masson said we did not evolve to have the family broken up but for anything but a fraction of each day. He also said that humans appear to be the only species that can consciously choose how involved they want to be as fathers.

### Animals imitate elders

"The beaver forms strong family bonds. The adults mate for life and have as many as six kits a year," wrote Hope Ryden, who spent four years observing a family of beavers. "The offspring from previous years make up a colony, and they spend the winter in a dark lodge sharing food from a common larder. They have developed certain social strategies: to care for each other, to communicate by sounds and bodily postures, and to have a high threshold for restraining themselves from expressing aggressive behavior."

She continued: "What intrigued me is that the beaver is capable of directing its social behavior to nonbeavers, and it sometimes forms relationships with human beings. The fact that beaver kits remain with their family for two years and sometimes longer certainly suggests that the young have something to learn from their elders. Beaver kits need role models to show them where and how best to use their innate building skills. The tendency of young animals to copy their parents has high survival value and ... the kits I observed imitated their elders."

# Chapter Five

# Valuing Awesome Nature

In the beginning God created...the earth...
Genesis 1:1 (*The Holy Bible*, The New International Version)

*Does the land belong to us?*

Mathew Fox and Rupert Sheldrake wrote, "...it takes a thousand years for God and nature to grow one inch of top soil."

Aldo Leopold wrote essays from a sand farm in Wisconsin, where his family tried to rebuild "with shovel and axe, what we are losing elsewhere. It is here that we seek and still find our meat from God."

Leopold believed some of us could live without wild things while there are some among us who cannot. He also wondered if the higher standard of living we seek is worth its cost in things natural, wild and free. For those us of the minority, the opportunity to see geese is more important than television and the finding of a wild flower is a right inalienable as free speech.

"Conservation is getting nowhere because it is incompatible with our Abrahamic concept of land," he wrote. "We abuse land because we regard it as a commodity belonging to us. When we see land as community to which we belong, we may begin to use it with love and respect. That land is a community is to be loved and respected is an extension of ethics. That land yields a cultural harvest is a fact long known but utterly forgotten."

Leopold felt that the world is too greedy in her pursuit of material things. He said "Perhaps a shift of values can be achieved by reappraising things unnatural, tame and confined in terms of things natural, wild and free.

"Ample recent evidence exists to support the contention that there are many who would pick apart the vital fabric of the in order to supply themselves with inessential luxuries. It is the same philosophy that concludes that when it comes time to cut timber, mine ores or dam rivers, well, sorry, but red-cockaded woodpeckers and others will just have to go. This is part of the belief that if we own the land it is our right to do anything we please with it."

We all agree that nature evokes an awed response. "How can one describe in words even a single plant, much less the teaming plant life of a swamp?" Leopold asked. "At times we make the mistake of thinking that plants are not alive, that they are just decorative props which create a matrix, a stage on which the lives of plants take place. To know plants is to know otherwise. In their own way, plants are as dynamic, as alive, as busy, as responsive as any animal."

### *We borrow the earth from our children*

An ancient Native American Proverb said, "Treat the earth well: it was not given to you by your parents, it was loaned to you by your children. We do not inherit the Earth from our ancestors, we borrow it from our children. When we Indians kill meat, we eat it all up. When we dig roots, we make little holes. When we burn grass for grasshoppers, we don't ruin things; when we build houses we only use dead wood. We don't chop down the trees."

*We need appreciation of earth*

According to Skutch, we most need more intense contemplation and a great enjoyment and appreciation of the beautiful natural world that surrounds and supports us. This natural world that surrounds us goes unnoticed in the narrow human world as we squander its resources in our we struggle for wealth.

"...only an appreciative human mind could bind all this diversity together in an act of grateful acknowledgement that lifts existence to a higher plane," he continued. "Widespread, adequate appreciation of our plant, now so undervalued and abused would not only contribute greatly to its health but bind people of all races and nations together in a shared purpose and ideal as nothing else could. Nobody with adequate appreciation of this plant's uniqueness, beauty and bounty would wage war, for such appreciation would override all greed for territory, power and wealth."

Skutch railed against the havoc that modern technological warfare wreaks upon nature. No matter which side wins the war, the planet loses. The world's resources are drained—wastefully. Forests are sacrificed to supply timbers for military purposes; its minerals are also sacrificed for armaments and ships that may be soon destroyed; oil from sunken vessels pollute oceans; high explosives scar the face of the earth; and chemicals poison it, including radioactive substances.

"All nature suffers when nations, forgetting what they owe to Earth that supports them, attack each other with barbaric fury."

Skutch recounted a parable that tells about three youths who lived in the shadow of a tall mountain covered with snow. The three challenged each other to a contest to prove their courage and stamina. Each was to climb the mountain alone and bring back some object that proved the heights of his climb.

The first three brought--in turn--an acorn, a pine cone, and an alpine flower. The fourth--who climbed the highest-

-came back with nothing because the snow he had collected on the highest peaks had melted as he returned. But he lived the rest of his life in a more thoughtful manner, a man whom neighbors sought for the wisdom he had gained because of having seen the view of the valleys and other mountains while at the mountaintop.

Skutch concluded, "This parable...reminds us that the chief values which we derive from wild nature cannot be held in our hands.

"Appreciative contemplation unites us ideally with all that excites our love or admiration and makes us feel less alone. A world so bound together by an appreciative mind is certainly superior to one in which everything exists only for itself. Widespread adequate appreciation of our planet, now so undervalued and abused, would not only contribute to its health but bind people of all races and nations together in a shared purpose and ideal as nothing else could. Nobody with adequate appreciation of his planet's uniqueness, beauty and bounty would wage war; such appreciation would override all greed for territory, power, and wealth," he concluded.

*Humans are not the zenith to all existence*

David Quammen visited Chile where damming the Futaleufu River was under consideration, which would flood an area of outstanding natural beauty. The plan would put most of the valley's agricultural land, most of its homesteads, and all of its great whitewater under a pair of reservoirs. It would also bury the road, cutting off the valley's fragile connection with the rest of the country. He asked if we must continue making our world everywhere flatter, tamer, simpler and uglier in order to take care of the population growth.

He believes that rivers can die, too, since they are animate. "To drown a river beneath its own impounded water, by damming it, is to kill what it was…. When the damming happens without good reason—simply because electricity is a product and products can be sold—then it's a tragedy of diminishment for the whole planet, a loss of one more wild thing…"

He wonders, for example, "if the citizens of Chile need more electricity and a short-term construction boom there? Or do they need spectacular wild places within their own country for their own spiritual refreshment and edification? "

"Humanity badly needs things that are big and fearsome and homicidally wild," he maintained. "We need to preserve those few remaining beasts, places and forces of nature capable of murdering us with sublime indifference. We need the tiger… the saltwater crocodile, and the grizzly bear…. and the Komodo dragon… for exactly the same reason we need the Futaleufu River; to remind us that homo sapiens aren't the unassailable zenith to all existence. We need these awesome entities because they give us perspective. They testify that God, in some sense or another, might not be dead after all."

"Wild places, in the ordinary sense of that phrase, are in preciously short supply on Planet Earth at the end of the twentieth century," he observed.

A man who opposed the project sent this e-mail to people around the world: "To dam this river would be like blowing up the Sistine Chapel."

### The earth is alive

"Step on the earth and your food presses down on over a thousand living creatures," wrote Elliott Minor. "According to a recent scientific study, in a square foot of ordinary topsoil an inch deep, there lurks and average of 1,356 living creatures …not to mention the microscopic population that would include up to two billion bacteria and million of fungi, protozoa, and algae."

"Nature," Rupert Sheldrake wrote, "which we have treated

as dead and mechanical, is in fact, alive. It is coming to life again before our very eyes." From the time of our remotest ancestors until the seventeen century, it was taken for granted that the world of nature was alive. But in the last centuries, growing numbers of educated people have come to think of nature as lifeless. "The mechanistic approach has provided us with technological and industrial progress; it has given us better means of fighting diseases; it has helped transform traditional agriculture into agribusiness and animal husbandry into factory farming; and it has given up weapons of imaginable power," he continued.

The approach of the mechanistic scientist, technocrat, economist, or he developer is based on the assumption, he observed, that natural resources are there to be developed, and their only value is the one places on them by market forces. Through the successes of technology, the mechanistic theory of nature is now triumphant on a global scale...it has become a kind of religion.

"The idea of a living nature...points toward a new kind of science, a new understanding of religion, and a new relationship between humanity and the rest of the living world...the whole of human history has involved man's domination of nature to varying degrees. What is unique in the modern world is not the fact of human power itself nor the sense of the uniqueness of humanity, but the vast increase in human power," he continued.

"The most dramatic example of this process was the opening of the American West," he wrote. "Into the abundant fertile lands of the west moved relentless waves of speculators and settlers. Before them retreated the wilderness and the native people who had lived so lightly on their land.... Between 1872 and 1874, over three million buffalo were hunted to supply them (for meat or pleasure). By 1880, though no one could believe it, the buffalo were gone...and now, like the buffalo hunters, we can hardly believe what we have done."

## We must cherish our wild places

Near midnight, photographer Annie Griffiths Belt quietly scaled a ridge in northeastern Alaska. Miles away, she could see 10,000 caribou moving across the tundra. The sight brought her to her knees. Before the Europeans arrived, North America teamed with herds of bison, elk antelope, deer, but even these caribou at the farthest corner of our continent are under siege from those who covet the potential petroleum reserves beneath heir hoofs. As Belts has worked for 25 years in every region of our nation, she has noticed that some of the purest remains have been saved by accident, such as in a cemetery. "As we urge the rest of the world to stop clearing rain forest, stop poaching save the whales... it would be wise to look is our own backyard. If we, who are blessed with an abundance of space, wealth, and education, can't cherish our own last wild places, then who can?"

## Changing the surface of the earth

Sigurd F. Olson said that man has devoted his intelligence and energy to conquering nature, subduing it, molding it to his will. He has in the last few decades changed the surface of the earth, crisscrossing it with a vast network of roads, excavations and lines of communication. He has become a geological force, leveling mountains, pushing hills into valleys, swamps, and estuaries, polluting the earth, air, and water to the point it may soon become uninhabitable for him, as well as all other species.

Olson believes that after man has exhausted the earth's resources, robbed both water and soil of nutrients, exterminated many forms of wildlife, and reached a point in his savage exploitation, he must assess what he has done.

*Water is the blood of the land*

"Water is the blood of a land, it courses through the internal seams and passageways of a continent, cleansing and carrying nutrients to all its farthest reaches," wrote Barbara Kingsolver. Yet, throughout our Nation's history, she observed, we have participated in the bloodletting; draining Southern marshes to raise crops, tapping aquifers and channeling rivers in the west to take care of the needs of ranchers and farmers; damning rivers, strangling the natural flow of water; harnessing water to meet our needs of transportation, power and waste removal. With regards to wetlands, Americans have looked on them as nuisances to be gotten rid of. "The desecration of the Florida everglades is a prime example," she observed. "Today the U.S has drained over half of its wetlands.

"Nothing calls out to the human psyche the way the ocean does. Our dams and dredging our removal of the land's natural cover to build homes of our own along the coastal edges of our continent, our ultimate need to concentrate our wastes and toxins and send them out to sea--these facts of our living have adversely affected the coastal watersheds. The toll is enormous," she concluded.

*The planet births itself*

"Earth is a water plane. It is a world of salt, oceans, cloud forest, underground springs, and winding rivers," wrote Karen Wright. "Everywhere water travels, life follows, between the earth and the earth's atmosphere, the amount of water remains constant, there is never a drop more or a drop less. This is the story of circular infinity, of a planet birthing itself. After I learned this, I watched the clear raindrops dropped out of the sky, falling to the earth. I was overwhelmed with the beauty of it. Our toxic world ever renews itself in its journey through earth and sky. "

"Half of the earth's animals live in the humid jungles (the

Amazon rainforest), most of them yet to be named, and plants that already transformed the history of modern medicine, plants used as treatments for leukemia and Parkinson's disease," wrote Linda Hogan. "These forests are the place our air is born, from a marriage of water and green-leafed dripping plants, in their verdant density, they produce over a fourth of the earth's oxygen."

## Rapid population is taxing rivers

In Tim Palmer's book, *Rivers of America,* he showcases over 200 photographs and essays showing the beauty and importance of rivers. Palmer said, "I used to sit alone by the river, breathing its sweet air. The spirit of the water poured into my soul and the rest of the world disappeared. When you think about it, our bodies are 70% water, and every drop comes from a river or ground water, so the rivers literally flow in our veins.

"When I went to college I studied landscape architecture and later I became a nature writer and photographer." His career led him to study rivers.

"Rapid population growth is taxing our rivers...urban sprawl, increased waste, and a growing demand for drinking water all disrupt and pollute water ways," Palmer continued: "The Colorado River is suffering its worst drought in a century., and in the spring of 2005, almost two dozen rivers and streams in Washington state were at record low levels. Learn about the river in your community. Go see it, take the kids, and talk with the people who are responsible for it. You will want to quickly learn what you can do to conserve and preserve it."

## The dying prairie

Every July, Aldo Leopold kept his eye on a country graveyard established in the 1840's in Wisconsin. There, a yard of silphium that had yellow blossoms resembling sunflowers burst into bloom. That patch of silphium might have been the sole remnant of the

plant on which the buffalo grazed when our country was young...
in the western half of the United States. One summer the flowers
bloomed on July 24, later than usual. On August 3, he drove past
and felt despair when he saw that a road crew had removed the
fence and mowed the flowers. He predicted the flowers would
try to revive for a few years and then give up, "With it will die
the prairie epoch."

The erasure of a human subspecies is largely painless to us
if we know little enough about it. We grieve only for what we
know. The erasure of silphium from western Dance County is
no cause for grief if one knows its name only in a botany book.
Leopold tried of dig some of the silphium up to move to his farm
but did not succeed because of the plant's tenacious root system.
After that he planted seeds that came up quickly, but after five
years they had still not borne a flower stalk. That made him
wonder about the age of the plant in the cemetery; was it older
than the cemetery itself? "Few grieved when the last buffalo left
Wisconsin and few will grieve when the last silphium follows him
to the lush prairies of the never-never land," Leopold wrote.

*The corn speaks*

Vickie Herme wrote about Barabara McClintock's work with
animals in *Adam's Task,* in which McClintock advocated that
people must take the time to look and the patience to hear what
each organism has to say to us. "We were told by the creator, this
is your land, keep it for me until I come back," McClintock said,
quoting a Native American elder.

McClintock, a biologist who received the Nobel Prize for her
work on gene transportation in corn plants, would listen to what
the corn had to say, then would translate it into human language.
She came to know each plant as an individual, seeing all plants as
alive. She developed a respect for life that allowed her to see more

deeply into the mysteries of matter than did other geneticists who worked on the same problems.

## When will our barbarians come?

Sigurd F. Olson believed that we are on the verge of making the greatest decision of all, a change in the goals and philosophies that brought about the present ecological crises, a complete realignment of our relationship to the earth. He believed that, at last, we are beginning to understand what is at stake. It is more than wilderness, beauty, or peace of mind; it is the survival of man and his culture. He pointed to other ages that have passed into oblivion, such as what happened to the fertile lands of Mesopotamia and the hundred dead cities built one of top of the other, the eleven civilizations that simply disappeared, to realize it was not war or pestilence that brought their end, but changing climates, unwise use of the land, and lack of vision. "It was then the barbarians moved down from the mountains to destroy the cities for the people were weakened and had no strength or will to repel disaster," he wrote.

## Chapter Six

## How Animals Help Us

...for every animal of the forest is mine,
and the cattle on a thousand hills.
I know every bird in the mountains,
And the creatures of the field are mine.
...for the world is mine, and all that is in it.
Psalm 50: 10, 11, 12b (*The Holy Bible*,
New International Translation)

*Zen masters*

"I have lived with many Zen masters," wrote Eckhart Tolle, "all of them cats."

*A dog heals*

Sally, a psychotherapist who said she's "not even a dog person," told me this experience she had when she became a member of a group of Vietnam widows who organized to help someone who loses someone who was on military duty. Soon after the attacks on the twin towers in New York on September 11, 2001, she saw a powerful example of the power of dogs to heal people. After those attacks, Sally went to help Pentagon families cope with their experiences. She was directed to sit at a table in a mezzanine in a hotel in Washington, D.C. She was to be "available to talk" to survivors. Every day, eight therapy dogs wearing red bandanas identifying who they were, stood with their owners, on hand also to help.

Sally had never seen those dogs in action before. As she watched, she saw a woman walking around, looking at the floor, in an obvious state of shock. A yellow lab looked at his owner and pulled on his leash, indicating, "Let me go." The woman had stopped walking and stood with an expression of extreme pain on her face. The dog stopped in front of the woman and looked at her. She did not respond. The dog then sat, holding steady eye contact with the woman. When the woman acknowledged the dog, he leaned into her leg. The dog sat on his haunches, still looking at her. She then knelt in front of him, hugging him. He leaned on her shoulder, and she began to sob. She sobbed for a long while. "This was one of the most therapeutic lessons I ever learned," Sally said.

## The old man and his true friend

A man had been a lumberjack in Washington and Oregon, placing often in grueling lumberjack competitions. At 67, a heart attack stopped all strenuous activity, wrote Angela Hynes. His daughter invited Dad to live with them on their small farm. She soon regretted the invitation because her father criticized everything. Rick sought help from their pastor who set up weekly counseling sessions for the couple. The pastor closed each session with a prayer that God would soothe the old man's troubled mind. As the days wore on, Catherine--who believed in a Supreme Being who had created the universe but had difficulty believing that God cared about the tiny human beings on this earth--got tired of waiting for a God who did not answer. She called mental health clinics, asking for suggestions. One employee told her of a study done at a nursing home that reported that depressed patients' attitudes had improved dramatically when they had a dog.

Catherine drove to the local animal shelter that afternoon.

No dog caught her eye until she came face-to-face with an old pointer. The employee told her that the dog had appeared at their gate two weeks before and that if no one claimed him by the next day, he would be put to sleep. Catherine drove the dog home and called out to Dad that she had brought him a dog. Dad rejected "that old bag of bones" with a wave of his arm and walked toward the house. The dog pulled from her grasp, wobbled toward Dad, sat before him, then slowly raised his paw. Dad stared at the uplifted paw while his lower jaw trembled. The pointer waited, then Dad dropped to his knees and hugged the animal. Dad spent countless hours with the dog whom he named Cheyenne.

The two were inseparable for three years as Dad's bitterness faded. In the middle of the night, Cheyenne waked Catherine and Rick with his cold nose. Dad had died. Cheyenne died three days later. At Dad's funeral, the pastor's eulogy paid tribute to Dad and to the dog who changed his life. He read from Hebrews 13:2: "Be not forgetful to entertain strangers...."

*The Pet Prescription*

Dr. Mehmet Oz said, "I'm excited about the mountain of evidence that pets can improve our physical well-being." Here's a list of ways they help:

*Reduced risk of allergies, asthma and eczema.* A surprising study showed that this immune-stabilizing effect appears to begin before birth. Prenatal pet exposure lowers allergic antibody production in the umbilical cord.

*Lower blood pressure.* "The simple act of petting an animal—or even gazing at an aquarium—results in a drop in blood pressure," Dr. Oz said.

*A stronger heart.* Dog owners have only a 1 percent change of dying within a year after a heart attack. Owning a cat made owners 37 percent less likely to die of a heart attack than those who hadn't.

*Improved fitness.* Dog owners are more likely to walk the recommended minimum 150 minutes of exercise per week.

*Greater calm for Alzheimer's patients.* These patients have fewer anxious outbursts if an animal is present, and caregivers can feel less burdened as well.

Dr. Oz recommends that if it's not possible for you to own a pet, volunteer with rescues. Go to petfinder.com to look up shelters near you.

"Pets are linked to improvements in the health and survival of patients with heart disease," wrote Pam Hillinger. "Animal companionship can reduce blood pressure, pulse and respiratory rates among both children and adults." She reported that a 1991 Australian study not only revealed decreases in blood pressure, but decreases in triglycerides and cholesterol among pet owners. Dog owners enjoyed better psychological and physiological health over the term of the study than those who did not own pets.

## Mind/body effects of dealing with animals

Backyard chickens are now the rage in cities and burbs, especially in the South. Why is the South so taken with chickens? For one reason, "Backyard chickens make great additions to the family," wrote Carolyn Llorens. She said that they help her husband, Hector, relax after a hard day. "He'll grab a martini, walk out in the yard, and just watch the chickens. For him, it's total stress relief."

Perhaps the biggest benefit for families with chickens is the chance to open children's eyes to the cycle of life from egg to chick to hen and back to egg. "It's a very ground experience for them; they see where life comes from and also where food comes from. They start to realize what an animal goes through to produce food for us," said Jimmie Henslee. "Children who grow up with chickens learn to be gentler with creatures. Hopefully, this will lead to more humane treatment for all animals."

Angela Hynes wrote about the mind/body effects of dealing with animals: reduced blood pressure, heart rate, and cholesterol; reduced triglyceride levels; reduced stress; reduced depression; and fewer visits to a doctor. Growing up in a home with a pet can lower infants' likelihood of developing allergies as they older; and some anecdotes suggest that dogs can predict the onset of seizures and detect bladder cancer.

Hynes wrote about Joan Mehew, director of the Dolphin Research Center in Grassy Key, Florida, where programs run to enrich the lives of both children and adults with special needs, reported that interacting with dolphins increases these individuals' self-esteem. Dolphins adjust their speed of movement to accommodate the disabilities of the people.

Hynes reported about the work that psychotherapist Marlena Deborah McCormick, Ph.D. and her parents, Thomas E. and Adele Von Rust McCormick, have pioneered, using horses to treat emotionally disturbed teens and adults. Adele McCormick, a sensitive person, coaxed a mute, withdrawn young man to interact with a horse. That interaction changed the man's life. McCormick and her parents changed the way they practice psychiatric medicine because of what they observed. "We began to see that nature, and the horse in particular, is able to reach people in a profound way," she noted. "Horses center people because in their presence you must be still," she said. "They respond negatively to people who are too hyper." Interaction with the horses teaches people how to improve their nonverbal communication skills and to have a greater sense of authority that they can use in their everyday lives. "The authority you have with horses can't be from any rhetoric," she explained. "It has to be authentic or the horse won't respond. For most of us, animals bring out our nurturing and protective natures and make us feel more responsible," Hynes observed. "We are touched not only by the companionship and cuddle factors, but by the unwavering loyalty and lack of guile."

*Mourning doves*

"Shortly after my mother's passing," Okeh Jean Bird wrote, "Dad stopped by for some company. He enjoyed sitting on our back deck watching the many birds that visit our feeders. That day, a mourning dove seemed to realize Dad's heart was heavy. It walked up to him, flew onto his knee and kept him company for about 15 to 20 minutes. The bird preened itself, then tucked its head under its wing for a short nap. My husband witnessed the whole episode. While it's hard to believe, it was as though this little bird tried to console Dad during a difficult time. Now you know why they're called "mourning doves"."

*Gifts from the sea*

Steven Callahan, adrift at sea alone for 76 days, speared fish to eat to stay alive. Approximately 36 dorados "escorted" him along the way. One day, he aimed at one and missed. "Again. Hit. A fine female," he wrote. "Lifted up, she glints in the sun. Her body pulses. She curls her head toward her tail-left side, right side, left, right, faster and faster. My delicate lance sways to her rhythm. What a magnificent animal. In one smooth move that has become instinctive, I swing inside and finish her off. Again I am provided with a buffer against starvation. Again I'm saddened by the loss of a companion. More and more, I feel that these creatures exude a spirit that dwarfs mine. I don't know how to explain it rationally--perhaps that's the point. I don't think that these fish reflect or think as we do; their intelligence is of a different kind. Now I find that is more the other way around. It is my ability to reason that keeps command and allows me to survive, and the things I am surviving for are those that I want by instinct: life, companionship, comfort, play. The dorados have all of that here, now. How I wish I could become what I eat."

As he concluded his book, he expressed his gratitude to the

sea. Although the sea was his greatest enemy, it was also his greatest ally. He knew intellectually that the sea is indifferent, but her richness allowed him to survive. In giving up her dorados, she was giving up her own children, so to speak, in order that he might live.

## Scratching a dog's belly

An anonymous person contributed this item to "The Vent" column in *The Atlanta Journal-Constitution:* "I figure that every time I reach down to pet my dog or scratch his belly, I add three weeks to both our lives. One day, science will prove this to be true, but in the meantime, it's an honor to be a part of the research."

# Chapter Seven

# Nature's Spiritual Influences

I lift up my eyes to the hills—
Where does my help come from?
My help comes from the Lord,
the maker of heaven and earth.
Psalm 120: 1, 2 (*The Holy Bible*, New International Translation)

### God's fantastic creation

A young mother was reading her five-year-old daughter, Amanda, the story of creation from the Bible, wrote B. J. Funk. At the end of each grand creation, the mother read, "And God saw that it was good."

Finally, Amanda stopped her mother and exclaimed, "That's all? God just said it was *good?* After doing all of that, he didn't say it was *fantastic?* It was *wonderful!*"

### Getting a glimpse of the face of God

Steven Callahan, lost at sea 76 days alone, wrote, "…to go to sea is to get a glimpse of the face of God."

### God is everywhere

Rick Bass, who moved to a remote valley of thirty inhabitants, the last valley in Montana without electricity, drove literally to the last road in the United States, a grave-and-dirt road that paralleled the Canadian border. He wrote, "There are days that I promise, when I swear, that as long as I can walk up the trail behind the house, or as long as I can go out into the yard and look up at the stars, I'll never be unhappy, never, I'll not just count by blessings, but shout them."

One night he and his daughter Elizabeth watched a particularly beautiful display of the Northern Lights. "The northern lights—green and yellow—came out around midnight," he wrote. "They shone over the tops of the mountains like the announcement of a strange Broadway opening. Then they began to shoot, in streaks and flashes—and rolling, too, like fast rivers—across the sky, right over our heads. We stayed out and watched them for an hour and a half, before they faded and then disappeared."

He said: "This valley shakes with mystery, with beauty, with secrets, and it gives up no answers. I sometimes believe that this valley--so high up in the mountains, and in such heavy woods, is like a step up to heaven...the last place you go before the real thing.

"There's a strange thing about myself that I can't explain. When I walk in the woods, if it's not snowing, I feel like what I am—a man. But if snow's falling—heavily, with that underwater hush everywhere—I feel like an animal.

"A driving snowstorm, big flakes blowing past, crashing into the woods, swirling in the meadows. They are the currency of winter, and I am the richest man in the world," he confessed.

At another time, he and his daughters hiked through the old forest along a rushing creek near their home. "We walked for a long time, passing through shafts of late-afternoon summer light filtering in beams and columns down through the latticework branches of old cedars, falling softly through the feathers of the old larch." Later in the day, on the walk back, the four-year-old... asked, seeming out of nowhere, "Where is God?"

"Everywhere," Rick answered.

*Wilderness is spiritual*

Tom Brown, Jr. wrote that his brother Rick asked Grandfather (a Native American teacher), what good it was live in the wilderness.

"It is in the purity of the wilderness that we must learn, free from the distractions of man," Grandfather answered. "It is the wilderness that brings us closer to the creator and to the realities of life. It is not a world built by the hands of men, or influenced by the laws of society. Once the learning process in the wilderness is over, a man must make frequent journeys into the world of man to share with them what is taught by the wilderness. There is a consciousness found in nature that seems to seep into the very soul. It becomes a cleansing, healing, and awakening, as if all the rush and turmoil of life is washed away and there is nothing but purity. I don't believe that anyone can walk in the wilderness without casting off the burdens of life…for nowhere is one closer to the creator than in the temples that his hands have made."

Most of what Grandfather taught were the things of the spirit. "Grandfather believed that the greater part of man's existence was in the spiritual realms and flesh was only a small part of man's life," wrote Tom Brown of his time spent with Grandfather. "He believed in the duality of all things, where at once we walked in flesh and at the same time in spirit. He also believed in the oneness of all things where at once we were part of Creation, and Creation was part of us, where our lives flowed through the life of the planet, Earth Mother, and Earth flowed through us and out of wilderness…."

The more Brown searched, the more he lived in wilderness, the more power he found in what Grandfather had taught. Now, journeying from wilderness and into the realms of society, he has found these teachings have become even more real. He sees a society which is crumbling, a society that lives mostly in the flesh, and knows little of the spirit. He sees a people lost and searching for themselves, not knowing which way to turn to find a spiritual path in life. And he sees a world that is quickly entering its final winter, where life on this planet as we now know it to exist will quickly come to an end. All he knows is that physical change is not enough. The global society must have a complete change, which includes a shift in consciousness to that of the spirit. Man must come back to the Earth and understand he cannot live above the laws of Creation, for now we are on borrowed time.

## Cutting our spiritual roots

Sigurd F. Olson wrote that, following the industrial revolution, the entire civilized world was changed. In the process, he observed that man had cut his spiritual roots to the land and to the interdependencies that over the centuries had preserved the ecosystem of which he was once an integral part. He maintained that we must find a balance between technology and preserving the environment.

## Spend time each day in nature

In *Inner Simplicity,* Elaine St. James said that many cultures throughout history have thought of nature as an integral and necessary part of their inner lives. Our society, on the other hand, has lost contact with the restorative, healing and inspirational power of the great outdoors.

"Make spending time with nature an important part of your spiritual pursuits," St. James said. "If walking is included in your daily regimen, make sure that in addition to the exercise and fresh air benefits of being outdoors, you also connect on an inner level with the beauty of the sun and the sky and the earth."

She advocates that we start each day with a deep, invigorating breath of fresh air, and an appreciation of the weather, no matter what it's doing. She said that we are to make a point to delight in the trees and birds and flowers and plant life on our route.

"Before you get into your car or hop onto the train...notice the patterns of the clouds...or the dew on the grass," she wrote.

"When weather permits," she continued, "have your lunch outdoors on a park bench, or on the grass under the shade of a tree, and use the time to quietly commune with nature."

She suggested that before going to bed at night, step outside for a few minutes. ...enjoy a deep breath of fresh air and get lost in a silent, meditative look at the night sky.

For those who live in the city, she urged that people go to parks or other places on weekends.

## Mystery of the monarchs

"This...question--how do monarchs find their way back to the same oyamel trees year after year? remains one of the great-unsolved mysteries of animal biology," wrote Sue Halpern. "Monarchs are not guided by memory, since no single butterfly ever makes the round trip. Three or four generations separate those that spend one winter in Mexico from those that go there the next."

## Caring for plants meet spiritual needs

Andrew Young, former mayor of Atlanta and ambassador to the UN, now raises bonsai.

In 1988, a local nursery official gave him a juniper bonsai, which he still has. That same year, while attending the Seoul Olympics, he saw a bonsai exhibit in connection with the Games. He made his first purchase from a Seoul horticulturist—a boxwood—and left the man $500 along with a request for him to send as many plants as that amount of money would buy.

Young has continued with that hobby, keeping enough trees thriving to feel some confidence and has buried enough to remain humble.

He has reaped a great deal of personal satisfaction from the hobby. A longtime associate and family friend said that the hobby "had a very calming, relaxing effect" on Young during stressful times. "When you're tending bonsai plants you really can't think about anything else but what you're doing."

Young is in the grip of "bonsai pleasure." He has learned patience by waiting for weeks for an apparently dead plant to show signs of life. It could take years for him to watch a forest of miniature maples to become a forest.

"Those little simple routines (watering, pruning, snipping) do something for your life," said Young. "It's like feeding the dog, taking out the garbage. It provides a certain basic routine, along with brushing your teeth, combing your hair…. That helps keep you sane."

Young is an ordained minister who has pastored churches along the way. He said: "We normally develop a pattern that meets our spiritual and emotional needs, as well as our physical needs. I don't think you could survive without it. That's civilization."

*Planet supports our spirit*

"The preparation of our planet…was an immensely long process…. Conceivably, the planet might supply everything necessary for the physiological processes of a large animal while offering little for its spiritual or intellectual development…. On our planet it has been otherwise; while developing an environment fit to support man's body, it has simultaneously prepared itself to nourish his spirit most generously….," wrote Alexander Skutch.

"A few generations ago, men of European origin especially in the New World, were exploiting the vegetable and animal kinds with little regard for anything except their own profit and pleasure…. Now…people almost everywhere are awakening to the fact that such reckless exploitation cannot continue without preparing great hardships for future generations…for it is undermining the very foundations of human life…."

Skutch pointed out that our relations with nonhuman creatures as constitute not simply an economic problem but also an ethical problem. We are certain that our treatment of animals and plants falls properly within the purview of ethics because, in addition to affecting the welfare of living things, it subtly affects the character of the actor, as is true of every act that has moral overtones. Kind and generous treatment of nonhuman creatures exalts and expands the spirit; callousness or cruelty to them...causes its further deterioration. "When we approach nature ethically, we are interested not only in how our treatment of living things affects them, considered as ends in themselves, but in what it does to the human spirit," Skutch concluded.

## A Man's Journey to Find Himself

"This book is about this magnificent cat and my lived-adventures tracking him in the Everglades, the eerie parallels to my Vietnam experiences, the swamp itself, and my quest to help save the cat from extinction--and also one man's journey to find himself," wrote James P. McMullen.

Prior to writing the book, he spent the last eight years tracking the panther in the part of the United Sates that is most like the Vietnam coastline and tropical jungle. For him, the war in Vietnam was a time of cruel disillusionment beyond all conception. "In my journey to manhood I participated in one of man's cruelest attempts at destroying half a country and thousands of people," he continued.

He mused that maybe he took on the personal responsibility of saving an endangered species on the verge of extinction because he found out first-hand what such a creature must feel like. Having been a part of destruction and death was a stepping stone to becoming an extreme preservationist. "I was hunted by the Viet Cong, preyed upon, and finally almost killed," he recalled. He considers it a miracle that he survived. He thinks that miracles have a purpose. He knows that the miracle of his own survival was what brought him to the Everglades.

He believes that it's a miracle that any panthers have survived, too. He wonders if maybe the purpose of that miracle is to make us consider our own survival as a species. He thinks that will be the biggest miracle of all.

It was the big cat that taught him peace, and a means of dealing with his life. The panther ultimately led him to God. Now he is never closer to Him than when he is in the swamp close to panthers. In their spirit territories, he and the panther were seeking each other. "Either way, our tryst was my wilderness rebirth as a human being into a new life, a life that offers itself as solid hope for the preservation of the Everglades, which has become the symbol of all wildness throughout the world," he wrote. "It was the panther that purred into my consciousness an infinite, positive power that made me realize that this big cat is much, much more than a wild animal on the prowl for prey." He sees the panther as a mysterious messenger.

McMullen bought a rifle, and out there in the swamp, he saw a blackbird on a bare limb. With a mechanical, unthinking act, he raised the rifle, aimed and shot, shooting the bird in half. He rushed up to it and saw its guts spread out in the mud. McMullen later asked himself what made him shoot that helpless bird. He vomited as he realized it was the most repulsive, worse thing he had ever done in his entire life. He had zapped it for no reason, no reason at all. It messed him up. He stood crying, picking the bird up, trying to put it back together and let it fly way. He wanted so badly for it to be alive. He has never picked up a weapon since then.

He came upon a Great White Eagle in the Everglades. "Suddenly, in a graceful silent ascent, he dove from the tree, flapped his wings and rose above the swamp, catching the wind, floating up in it, dissolving into the brightness of the sun as though a huge veil had opened up," he wrote. But against that brilliance, he did not see just a bird disappearing. What he saw was the timeless symbol of mankind that would never go extinct. "What I saw was a white eagle, the Great White Eagle, that deep in the heart everyone sees. It was no revelation to understand what was happening with this eagle. For it happens with all who dare to probe the mysteries of the wilds. The great White Eagle is in all of us, in every soul, every cell, every thought. The White eagle is mankind's supreme spiritual victory over himself. Anyone can look at an eagle, but those who dare to look within, to probe that eagle's soul, find their own souls," he concluded.

## Who gives and who takes?

"The Lord giveth, and the Lord taketh away, but He is no longer the only one to do so. When some remote ancestor of ours invented the shovel, he became a giver; he could plant a tree; and when the axe was invented, he became a taker, he could chop it down," Douglas Wood wrote. "Whoever owns land has thus assumed, whether he knows it or not, the divine functions of creating and destroying plants. I have read many definitions of what a conservationist is, and written a few myself, but I suspect that the best one written is not with a pen but with an axe. It is a matter of what a man thinks about while chopping, or while deciding what to chop. A conservationist is one who is humbly aware that--with each stroke--he is writing his signature into the face of the land."

"I'm sure there are many things I'll never learn from traveling over the earth by canoe," he continued. "I'm just not sure any of them are worth much.

"There is no finer subject for a picture than a pine," he noted. "But, the pine is the better artist; it paints pictures of the wind."

Wood lists the following to help us have a memorable life:
Attend sunrises.
Don't chase butterflies; be still, they'll land on you.

## Dogs teach us forgiveness

"Some men learn about forgiveness by studying the lives of saints," wrote C. W. Gusewelle. "And some of us keep dogs."

# Chapter Eight

# What Can We Do?

The earth is the Lord's, and the fullness thereof;
the world, and all they that dwell therein.
Psalm 24:1 (*The Holy Bible,* King James Version)

## Irresponsible humans

"It was probably always too much to believe that human beings would be responsible stewards of the planet," wrote Jeffrey Kluger. "We may be the smartest of the animals, endowed with exponentially powers of insight and abstraction, but we are animals all the same. That means we can also be shortsighted and brutish, hungry for food, resources, land and heedless of the mess we leave behind trying to get them."

## Some things people are doing

### Paint sent to poor nations instead of landfill

"Rony Delgarde, a Haitian native, founded Global Paint for Charity, a nonprofit organization that collects leftover paint free of charge and, instead of tossing it into landfills, uses it for good," wrote Gracie Bonds Staples.

In 2010 Delgarde was struck by the number of unpainted schools, churches, and homes he saw on a visit to Uganda and Kenya. When he returned, he founded his company, distributing paint across the globe.

To date, Global Paint Charity has distributed some 6,000 gallons new and used gallons of paint to Kenya, Uganda and Guinea, where he helped paint an orphanage for children who lost their parents to HIV/AIDS.

The charity will accept any container of latex or oil paint, regardless of the amount, age or condition. The goal, Delgarde said, is not only to offer pride to residents in developing countries but protect the environment and relieve donors of the burden of the burden of disposing of unused paint. The organization may be reached at globalpaints.org or at 678-314-3521 or 855-853-7772.

## Green companies

When a business with more than 7,000 stores, 1.8 million employees and $45 billion in sales changes it ways, then it is hard not to notice, wrote Jeffrey Kluger. Wal-mart has made itself the darling of the greens with its pledge to install solar panels, switch to hybrid vehicles, conserve water and even buy wild caught salmon. But Wal-Mart is not alone. Alcoa and Caterpillar, among others, asked the Federal Government to act aggressively on climate change and their amount of carbon dioxide emissions. "It took generations to foul up the planet as badly as we have, and it will take generations to reverse things. The difference is, we had the leisure of beginning our long industrial climb whenever we wanted to. We don't have the leisure of waiting around to clean up after it," Kluger said.

## What we can do

## Start a community garden

In the past decade, the once thriving manufacturing community of Lenoir, N.C. has experienced factory closings, losing 8,000 jobs. Many residents can't afford fresh food, and two-thirds of the town's adults and one-third of its children are overweight or obese.

Sara Mursch, 76, a retired air force nurse and longtime gardener, came up with the idea of a community garden. She pitched the idea to a few fellow gardening enthusiasts from her church, and they pitched the idea to the city manager, who donated a half-acre plot for $1 a year along with city workers to help clear and terrace the hilly, weed-filled land.

"The first garden was so successful that in spring 2010 another one, spanning 5.6 acres, was added across town on the site of a burned out factory," wrote Kate Meyers." In the three years since the gardens were established, eyesores have been transformed into plots bursting with lettuces, onions, squash, okra, and other vegetables. Today, there are nearly 100 beds.

Across the country, Meyers added, an estimated one million community gardens are blooming.

*A quiet, reflective and peaceful place*

In Atlanta, Nancy Jones has spent the past dozen years cobbling together green space in the north of the city for the animals who live there and the people who visit.

"Jones is executive director of the Blue Heron nature Preserves, a 25-acre ribbon of mature trees, wetlands and trails along Nancy Creek off busy Roswell Road and not far from busy Chastain Park," wrote Anne Hardie. "Despite its highly trafficked location and the fact that it is open to the public from dawn to dusk, Blue Heron remains largely unknown, except to the deer, beavers, otters, minks, wild turkeys, quails, pileated woodpeckers, and of course, the blue herons who call it home."

"Over the years, Jones and her allies in a civic association and the city have fended off developers."

Jones didn't plan to start a preserve. She could see the area from her front yard and loved walking the streams. "Then when the property was facing destruction from development, it really galvanized me to get involved," she said. She spent the next 12 years trying to connect other pieces and grow something. "I learned very quickly that, if you saw green space and you weren't thinking ahead, it was gone."

Jones said that her group is laying down a really good seed bank for trees and plant to prosper. "The animals are really important in the larger environmental sense," she said. "The coyotes keep urban rodents, like rats, down. Beavers restore water quality." The group also partners with Oglethorpe University for research. A retired art teacher, Jones started education classes at Blue Heron.

*Gardens blooming at schools*

Moss Haven's Elementary School's garden in Dallas, Texas is among a growing number being planted in schoolyards across the country. It is part of an American Heart Association initiative to get kids to eat healthier. Along with nutrition, school gardens also can teach lessons about the environment and science, teamwork, math skills and leadership, proponents say.

"The main thing that I really like is citizenship—that everybody is taking responsibility," said Ashley Rich, who works with teachers to develop curriculum at the school. Over the summer, families from the school have been taking turns each week caring for the garden.

"If the children are involved in growing the vegetables, then they are interested in eating them," said Judith Collier-Reid, national consultant for the Dallas-based American Heart Association's Teaching Gardens program, which has handed grants to about 160 gardens since kicking off last year. Its mission is to help curb the nation's childhood obesity epidemic.

Todd LoFrese, assistant superintendent for support services for Chapel Hill-Carrboro City Schools in North Carolina, said there's a gardening component at nearly all of their 18 schools. A new elementary school set to open next year has been designed to include garden plots and will have a rainwater collection system and a green roof with vegetation.

### Savannah: How does your garden grow?

In the heart of east Savannah, a community garden has helped supply one of the city's poorer neighborhoods–one without a close grocery store—with fresh vegetables and fruits. The garden is helping a new city program take root in other neighborhoods. The program would allow more than 1,250 city-owned parcels to be made available to residents or neighborhood associations to start community gardens.

The advantages, city officials believe, include beautification, exercise, providing healthier eating options and giving neighbors a chance to get to know each other while gardening. The gardens could also be a powerful motivator for street-corner teens who have no activities to occupy their time.

### The softening presence of trees

The presence of trees will soften a massive housing development in Atlanta, Georgia that will include 1,000 single-family homes, 780 apartments and an 18-hole golf course. Most of them were planted more than 45 years ago, when a now-demolished public housing project was developed.

Thanks to a community activist, Jackie Echols, who worked with Atlanta City Councilwoman Felicia Moore, those trees might have been removed. The women negotiated an agreement with the general managing partner of the development who got his two partners to agree to the plan.

"It's been an enlightening process for me, and I frankly think that the development is turning out to be much better," said Noel Khalil, the general manager. "I really regret that I didn't make protecting the trees a part of the master plan initially."

The first 7 acres of the 152-acre site were planned with no consideration to the existing trees. That's when Echols and community leaders began to challenge the development and got the developers to protect the trees. I n addition to the trees that were part of the stream buffer, the agreement called for saving at least 20 percent of the trees on the remaining 145 acres.

"Having to work around the trees is more difficult than your standard development practices," Steve Brock, one of the partners, said. "It makes for a more beautiful development, but it's a little painful; but the end product is worth the extra effort." He called the trees "as picturesque as they can be" because they've been growing for more than 40 years with virtually no disturbance.

## Birthing butterflies

"Judy," who has BS degree in botany, who taught high school honors biology for 20 years, who has been a member of Audubon for 35 years, and who "reads every nature magazine I could get my hands on and watches every nature show I can find on TV," believes that it is obvious to any nature lover that everything in the environment is out of balance and if we are going continue to enjoy many of the species we have today, we need to try to restore some of what has been lost.

One of the things that she and "Ted", her husband (now deceased) did years ago, when they first bought their house— which they actually bought for the trees and wildlife habitat that came with it--was to certify their yard as a wildlife habitat with Audubon. That meant that they would try to provide the amenities that wildlife needs and not use substances that would harm wildlife.

"One of the concerns I have had," Judy said, "is the scarcity of butterflies. In reading about what they need to survive, I found that they need host plants for the larvae and most need nectar sources for the adults. Each species is very particular about both of these, although they are less picky about nectar sources than most."

To be able to provide nectar sources, she has planted a variety of flowering perennials and each year has planted a variety of annuals that are known to attract butterflies. But if they do not find host plants to lay their eggs on, no reproduction will occur. Judy chuckled at a side benefit: many bunnies have also enjoyed and reproduced in her garden.

She has seen very few monarchs in the yard in the many years she has lived there, so she planted milkweed seeds and now milkweed grows abundantly at the back of the garden; but no monarchs have found them. Last year, she procured mail order monarch larvae and raised them in a screened box on milkweed leaves. They formed beautiful chrysalises, and all were successful hatches—which she promptly released in the back yard. She saw them a few more times, but the butterflies did not reproduce in her yard. A butterfly expert told her that they do not return the way birds do (to where they were born), so if they cannot find their way to her yard in suburbia by going from milkweed to milkweed if she is not on a migration path, she will probably not have success with them.

Over the years, Judy has had great success with black swallowtail butterflies since she always has a lot of parsley and fennel in her garden. Soon in the summer, the plants have so many larvae on them that she worries they will "eat themselves out of house and home". At first, she just watched them and hoped for the best, but she also feeds birds and has a healthy population of insect eaters going over every plant in her yard every day. She found that, as soon as the larvae were large enough to be visible, they were likely to be bird food. She decided that, in the interest of raising more butterflies to replace those that had laid the eggs, she would bring them in and feed them and protect them until they turned into the gorgeous adults that she so loves to see in her garden. (Some call it "keeping them in protective custody"). One time, she had so many that she ran out of provisions, so she called the Nature Center. They had plenty of "food," so she took them there, and they "finished" the cycle for them.

"One of the most beautiful butterflies of all to me is the gulf fritillary," she said. "I am so blown away by the iridescent pearl spots on its underwings, its carefree flight, and its gorgeous orange and black coloration. I would always see the adults but did not have a host plant for the larvae. A friend offered to help me out and gave me seeds for purple passion flower vines last fall (commonly called mampop). I was very blessed to end up with twelve beautiful passion flower vines, but due to the overabundance of rabbits and chipmunks, I did not dare plant them in the ground, so I used tall plastic pots so they would not get eaten or dug up. I placed the pots in different places and several were near where I had planted zinnias. One day as I walked past them and inspected them, I saw the small larvae of a gulf fritillary on the vine. I was so busy that day and it was so small, I thought to find it the next day and maybe bring it in, but it was not there the next day—or, as I have figured out since, it was very good at hiding, and I probably just did not find it.

"About a week later, my daughter and I searched again for larvae and found two, more than an inch long. We were beyond excited and brought them into the house and put them into the box I had prepared. I brought in young fresh passion plant leaves for them to eat (which they prefer). We also separated the box so that they would not be tempted to feed on each other, as I have found some larvae do. Somehow, I could just not get them to settle down. They were decidedly determined to crawl up onto the screen. I finally turned out the lights and went to bed, satisfied they would not be able to leave the enclosure.

"In the morning, I brought in fresh young leaves and stems, but the larvae kept climbing up onto the screen and were obviously agitated. Finally, in desperation, I found that I could carry a pot with the vines growing up staking poles into the house and set it into an oversized stone jar. I put the larvae back into the plant and for at least two hours they crawled all over, seldom eating, but by noon, both seemed to be comfortable with their locations and just sat there doing nothing. I kept watching, nervously. At about 6 p.m., one of them started hanging down in a position that was obviously the right one to make a chrysalis. By 7:00, both got into that position. One chose a stem, and the other the bottom of a leaf. By morning, both were looking like dead leaves just as the picture in the butterfly guide book shows. Now, I am anxiously awaiting the emergence of two gifts from God, which I will joyfully return to nature!

"My garden doesn't look as pretty as it could since the books say that we should deadhead (break off the flowers) so that the plants will keep making more flowers, but I do not do that. More flowers might be beneficial, but I try to plant enough so that more will keep coming on. I don't break them off, since I love birds. Goldfinches, house finches and many other birds love the seeds. I find that four or five goldfinches may be feeding at once on the seeds found sitting on the cone flower plants, the zinnia and sunflower plants. It is such a joy to see them there feeding naturally rather than having to totally depend on the feeders. Also, it is a tremendous joy to see the ruby throated hummingbirds-- that have been chased away from the feeders--visiting the flowers that still have nectar.

"The last few years of drought have badly hurt our wildlife populations, since flowers cannot produce nectar in abundance when they are so water stressed. Also, all wild creatures need water, so providing water for wildlife is as important--or more important--than providing food.

"God made us in His image and entrusted the care of the rest of His creation to us. If we do not care for it as He has asked us to, we are not fulfilling the expectations He has of His children."

"Judy" found these websites to be helpful: www.sasionline. org/fritillary.html and www.elizabethssecretgarden.blogspot. com/2009/08gulffritillary-life-cycle.htm.

Or you may type in gulf fritillary butterfly or gulf fritillary caterpillars, etc. where you will find the sites and more.

These are just a few of the ways to conserve energy and the planet as mentioned in *Time Magazine.*

1. Turn food into fuel. Municipal waste, wood pulp and leftover grain and corn husk can all be turned into cellulosic ethanol. Experiments are in the works to haste to make something out of waste.

2. Get blueprints for a greenhouse. You can use solar electric heating systems, geothermal heat pumps and you can have floors and countertops from recycled materials.

3. Change your light bulbs; use energy saving light bulbs.

4. Ditch the McMansions. Oversize houses require the use of more energy. Buy a house with only the space you will need.

5. Hang up a clothesline. Over a lifetime, drying a T-shirt can send up to 9 pounds of carbon dioxide into the air.

6. Build a skyscraper. The Bank of America Tower is the greenest building in New York and it followed a green blueprint in its construction. Work with businesses that are going green.

7. Turn up the geothermal heat. This system taps into water that is a relatively stable 55 degrees and transfers that heat to warm the building in the winter and cool it in the summer

8. Look at vintage clothes. Visit high end consignment clothing establishments. Buying quality used garments

or swapping clothes with friends saves energy and materials used in producing new ones.

9. Let employees work closer to or from home. Let employees work in the office closest to their home or it they can work from home let the. Escaping rush hour traffic has its own reward.

10. Ride the bus. America is ready for a change; we are just waiting for bus and rapid transit to come closer to urban areas.

11. Live in a highrise or dense area. The closer we live together, we prevent urban sprawl and the need for more gas stations, strip malls and convenience stores to be built, therefore saving materials and energy.

12. Pay your bills on line. Direct deposits and bill paying online eliminates trips to the post office, bank, and places to pay bills.

13. Open a window instead of using the A/C on warm days. Caulk, weather-strip and insulate to save energy. Use the dishwasher only when it is full; wash clothes in cold water and turn down the thermostat on the water heater. At the end of the year your home will feel lighter because it has lost about 4,000 pounds of carbon dioxide.

14. Energy audit your home. How green is your home? A home energy audit, which most utility providers will do free of charge, will tell you what you can do to reduce the amount of energy your home uses.

15. Check the label. Buy energy saving appliances and use the energy saving cycle on them.

16. Skip the steak.... There are 1.5 billion cattle and buffalo on the planet. Global meat production is expected to double between 2001 and 2050. Given the amount of energy consumed raising, shipping and

selling livestock, a 16 ounce T-bone is like a hammer on a plate.

17. Use paper bags. Every year more than 500 billion bag are distributed and less than 3% of those are recycled. They can take up to 1,000 years to biodegrade in landfills that emit harmful green house gases. And, if you do bring home plastic bags, find a place to pass them on—to the local library, for instance. Better still, buy cloth tote bags to bring your groceries and other items home.

18. Support your local farmer. Buying food grown closer to home saves petroleum used in shipping food and helps support the local economy and using foods in season is better for you and the environment.

19. Plant a bamboo fence. It takes in lot of carbon dioxide and also prevents using materials to make fence materials that use energy.

20. Have a green wedding. Buy a cake from a bakery; buy local flowers, wine from a neighborhood brewery.... Consider your local wedding a gift to the planet.

21. Shut off the computer.... Screen savers are not energy savers. If you use your home computer four hours a day and turn it off when not is use, you could save about $70 a year.

22. Rake in the fall colors.... A leaf blower uses a pint of gas and oil in an hour.... Leaves can still be raked by hand, and you get the exercise.

23. End the paper chase.... Nine hundred million trees are cut down every year to make paper. Plant a tree, and use recycled paper.

24. Make your garden grow.... Use natural fertilizers, such as grass clippings that do not emit harmful gases or carbon dioxide.

25. Fill your car with passengers.... Have car pools for work or taking children to school events, ride with a neighbor to the store....Full cars mean fewer cars on the road.
26. Borrow from and lend to your neighbors.

And above all,
observe,
value,
protect,
spend time in,
enjoy
and learn from
the natural world.

# Bibliography

Ackerman, Diane. "We are all a part of nature," *Parade Magazine*, April 20, 2003, p. 6.

Ancient Native American Proverbs, "American Indian Quotations on Protecting our Environment," *NIEHS Kids' Pages*.

Anonymous, "The Vent," *The Atlanta-Journal Constitution*, August 26, 2003, p. B2.

Bainton, Roland H. *Here I Stand: A Life of Martin Luther*. NY: New American Library, 1977.

Barrios, Gregg, "The Nature of Sandra Cisneros," *Nature Conservancy*, Fall 2003, Vol. 53, No. 3, p. 12.

Bateson, Mary Catherine. "Into the trees" in *Sacred Trusts: Essays on Stewardship and Responsibility*, edited by Michael Katasis. San Francisco: Mercury House, 1993.

Bass, Rick. The Green Hours" in Olsen, W. Scott & Bret Lott, editors. *A Year in Place*. Salt Lake City: University of Utah Press, 2001.

*Winter: Notes from Montana*. Boston: Houghton Mifflin/Seymour Lawrence, 1991.

Bird, Okey Jean, "Mourning doves," *Birds & Blooms*, Greendale, WI: Reiman Media Group, 2002, Collectors Edition (31), p. 24.

Braxton, Viola Andrew. *My Days of Work and Play*. Self-published in Greensboro, NC by Viola Andrew Braxton, 1995.

Brothers, Dr. Joyce, "Environment, mood," *Marietta Daily Journal*, Feb. 27, 2003, p. B2.

Brown, Tom, Jr. *The Journey*. N.Y.: Berkley Books, 1992.

Callahan, Steven. *Adrift: Seventy-Six Days Lost At Sea.* N.Y: Ballantine Books, 1986.

Caputo, Robert. "Mother bear man," Washington, DC: *National Geographic,* March 2002, p. 62.

Chadwick, Douglas H. and Joel Sartore. *The Company We Keep: America's Endangered Species.* Washington, D.C.: National Geographic Society, 1995, 1996.

Chapelle, Davis. *Navigating the Tides of Change,* Gabriola, Island BC Vol .I xo, Canada, New Society Publishers, 2001.

Chase, The Rev. Edwin, "When dust is everywhere," *Wesleyan Christian Advocate,* May 2, 2003, p. 12.

Cleary, William. *How the Wild Things Pray.* Leavenworth, KS: Forest of Peace Publishing, 1999.

Conn, Lesley, "Savannah garden program grows," *The Atlanta Journal-Constitution,* Aug. 27, 2012, p. B3.

deWalls, Frans. *Good Natured: The Origins of Right and Wrong in Humans and Other Animals.* Cambridge, Massachusetts: Harvard University Press, 1996.

Diamond, Jared. *Collapse: How Societies Choose to Fail or Succeed.* NY: Viking Press, 2005.

Dukes, Anne. "Plants therapeutic at Wesley Woods," *Wesleyan Christian Advocate,* May 2, 2003, p. 3.

Eller, Daryn. "Flower power," *Victoria,* Atlanta, Ga., April, 2002, p. 61.

Feiler, Bruce. *Walking the Bible: A Journey by Land Through the Five Books of Moses.* NY: HarperCollins Publishers, 2001.

Flanders, Danny C. "Healing gardens: horticulture therapy takes root in diverse treatment programs," *The Atlanta Journal-Constitution,* July 7. 2004, p. B12.

Folkerts, George W. and Lucian Niemeyer. *Okefenokee.* Jackson, MS: University Press of Mississippi, 2002.

Fouts, Roger, *Next of Kin: What Chimpanzees Have Taught Me About Who We Are.* NY. William Morrow & Company, Inc., 1997.

Fox, Matthew and Rupert Sheldrake. *Natural Grace.* NY: Doubleday, 1996.

Fox, Matthew and Robert Sheldrake, "Science, consciousness and spirit," *Dialogue with Matthew Fox and Rupert Sheldrake*. London: Colet House, April 6, 2009.

Funk, B. J. "Have you noticed God's creation lately?" *Wesleyan Advocate*, January 23, 2004, p. 12.

George, Jean Craighead. *Julie*: NY: HarperCollins Pub., 1994.

Gilbert, Elizabeth. *The Last American Man*. N.Y. Viking: The Penguin Group, 2002.

Goodall, Jane and Marc Bekoff. *The Ten Trusts: What we must do to Care for the Animals We Love*. N.Y.: Harper San Francisco, 2002.

Gusewelle, C.W., *The Rufus Chronicle: Another Autumn*. N.Y.: Ballantine Books, 1998.

Haines, John. *The Stars, the Snow, the Fire: Twenty-Five Years in the Northern Wilderness*. Saint Paul: Gray Wolf Press, 1989.

Halpern, Sue. *Four Wings and a Prayer: Caught in the Mystery of the Monarch Butterfly*. N.Y.: Pantheon Books, 2001.

Hardie, Ann. "A very quiet, reflective and peaceful place," *Atlanta Journal-Constitution*, Aug. 19, 2012, p. B5.

Hardin, Kris L., "Symbols" in *Sacred Trusts: Essays on Stewardship and Responsibility* edited by Michael Katasis. San Francisco: Mercury House, 1993.

Harrison, Barbara. *Orangutan*. NY: Doubleday & Company, 1963.

Hearne, Vickie. *Adam's Task: Calling Animals by Name*. NY: Skyhorse Publishing, 2007.

Hemenway, Toby. *Gaia's Garden: A Guide to Permaculture*. White River Junction, Vermont: Chelsea Green Publishing, 2001.

Henslee, Jimmie, in "Dixie Chickens," *Southern Living*, Birmingham, AL: Vol. 47, No. 8, p. 92.

Hillinger, Pam, "State of Mind/Body Answers," Schwader, Marilyn, Editor. *A Guide to Getting It; Sacred Healing*. Portland, OR: Clarity of Vision Publishing, 2005.

Hogan, Linda. *Dwellings: A Spiritual History of the Living World*. NY: Simon & Schuster: A Touchstone Book 1995.

Hope, Ryden. *Lily Pond: Four Years with a Family of Beavers*. NY: Lyons & Buford, 1989.

Hynes, Angela. "The healing power of animals," *Natural Health Magazine*. NY: Weider Publications, LLC, A Subsidiary of American Media, Inc., March 2005, p. 71.

"Judy," "Birthing Butterflies," personal interview, Atlanta, GA, August 25, 2012.

Kingsolver, Barbara. "Last Stand: America's Virgin Lands." *National Geographic*, Washington, D.C., December 2002, pp. 11, 12, 15, 28, 92, 93.

Kluger, Jeffrey, "What Now?" *Time Magazine,* April 9, 2007, p. 67.

Lamberton, Ken. *Wilderness and Razor Wire.* San Francisco: Mercury House, 2000. Used by permission from author.

Lawrence, R. D. *The North Runner.* Pleasantville, N.Y.: *Reader's Digest Condensed Books*, Vol. 4, 1979.

Leopold, Aldo. *A Sand County Almanac.* NY: Oxford University Press, 1966.

Llorens, Carolyn in "Dixie Chickens," *Southern Living*, Birmingham, AL: Vol. 47, No. 8, p. 92.

Lopez, Barry. *Arctic Dreams: Imagination and Desire in a Northern Landscape.* NY: Charles Scribner's Sons, 1986.

Masson, Jeffrey Moussaieff. *The Emperor's Embrace: Reflections on Animals, Families and Fatherhood.* NY: Pocket Books, 1999.

May, Lee. Gardening Life. Atlanta, GA: Longstreet Press, 1998.

Meyers, Kate. "Field of Dreams," *Parade Magazine*, Aug. 19, 2012.

Minor, Elliott, "Rain has helped Georgia's butterfly population," *Marietta Daily Journal*, August 4, 2003, p. 1B.

McMullen, James P. *Cry of the Panther: Quest of a Species.* Englewood, FL: Pineapple Press, 1984.

Norris, Kathleen. *Dakota: A Spiritual Geography.* NY: Ticknor & Fields, 1993.

Olson, Sigurd F. *Reflections from the North Country.* NY: Alfred A. Knopf, 1976.

Oz, Dr. Mehmet, "The Pet Prescription," *O Magazine*, April 2012, pp. 68, 71.

Palmer, Tim. "Taking Care of our Rivers," *Natural Health Magazine. NY:* June 2007, p. 24.

Pascoe, Elaine. *The Ecosystem of an Apple Tree.* NY: The Rosen Publishing Group's PowerKids Press, 2003.

Peck, Lisa. "Gratitude," unpublished essay. Tucker, GA: 2007. Used by permission.

Quammen, David. *Wild Thoughts from Wild Places*. N.Y.: Scribner, 1998.

Rash, Ron. *The Cove*. NY: HarperCollins Publishers, 2012.

Ryden, Hope. *Lily Pond: Four Years with a Family of Beavers*. NY: William Morrow and Company, 1989.

Saporta, Maria. "Trees teach lesson at West Highlands," *The Atlanta Journal-Constitution*, June 21, 2004, p. E3.

St. James, Elaine. Inner Simplicity. NY: MJF Books, Fine Communications, 1995.

Schooler, Lynn. *The Blue Bear*. NY: HarperCollins Publishers, 2002.

Seabrook, Charles. "Birds learn to sing," *The Atlanta Journal-Constitution, July* 21, 2012, p. B2.

Shedrick, Daphene, from Gerry Ellis. *Wild Orphans*. NY: Welcome Books, 2002.

Sheldrake, Rupert. *The Rebirth of Nature: The Greening of Science and God*. N.Y.: Bantam Books, 1991.

Skutch, Alexander. *A Naturalist amid Tropical Splendor*. Iowa City: University of Iowa Press, 1987.

Spalding, Linda. *A Dark Place in the Jungle*. Chapel Hill, NC: Algonquin Books of Chapel Hill, 1999.

Staples, Gracie Bonds. "Paint sent to poor nations instead of landfill," *The Atlanta Journal-Constitutionl*, Aug. 20, 2012, p. D1.

Stengle, Jamie. "Gardens blooming at schools teach lessons," *Marietta Daily Journal*, Aug. 27, 2012, p. D4.

Stepakoff, Jeffrey. *The Orcha*rd. NY: Thomas Dunne Books, 2011.

Stewart, J. http//www.physics.edu8082/stewart/scied 397/brain.html for info on species extinction.

Straight, Susan. "Treasure Winter's Wonders," *Hallmark Magazine,* January/February 2007, p. 14.

Tickle, Phyllis. *The Graces We Remember: Stories From the Farm in Lucy: Sacred Days of Ordinary Time*. Chicago: Loyola Press, 1988.

Tolle, Eckhart. *Guardians of Being*. NY: New World Library, 1109.

Towery, Twyman. *Wisdom of Wolves: Leadership Lessons from Nature*. Napierville, Ill: SimpleTruths Press, LLC, 2009.

Tudino, Cristina, "The Nurture of Nature," *O Magazine*, June 2012, p. 116.

Walhberg, David. "Monkeys ape human emotion," *The Atlanta Journal-Constitution,* Sept. 18, 2003, p. A1.

White, Robb. *Death Watch.* NY: Bantum Doubleday Dell Books for Young Readers, 1973.

Winfrey, Oprah. "I know this for sure," *O Magazine*, NY: February 2004, p. 168.

Wood, Douglas. *Breathe the Wind, Drink the Rain: Notes on Being Alive.* Sartell, MN: Wind in the Pines Publishing Co., 22002.

*Fawn Island.* University of Minnesota Press, Minneapolis: 2001.

*Paddle Whispers.* Duluth: Hamilton Press, 1993.

Wright, Karen, "The wonder of water transport in trees still stumps scientists," *The Atlanta Journal-Constitution*, Sept. 1, 2002, p. D3, quoted from *Discover Magazine.*

# About the Author

Sara Hines Martin holds a bachelor's degree in English, a Master of Religious Education degree, and a Master of Science degree in counseling. She lives in Acworth, Georgia and works as a therapist in private practice in Kennesaw, Georgia.

She has been writing professionally for more than 50 years. She is currently writing *Loving Yourself as You Truly Are: and Loving Others as They Are.*

Ms. Martin has lived in two third-world countries and has traveled widely around the world. She is a strong environmentalist and believes that God has given us a clear mandate to be good stewards of the earth. "Time spent in nature is time well spent," she says.